PARENTS ON THE RUN

PARENTS

ON THE RUN

by

Marguerite and Willard Beecher

A   COMMON   SENSE   BOOK

FOR   TODAY'S   PARENTS

DEVORSS & COMPANY
BOX 550 • MARINA DEL REY • CALIFORNIA 90294

Library of Congress Catalog Card No.: 73-83773
ISBN: 0-87516-522-2

Originally published by The Julian Press, Inc., New York,
and subsequently by Galahad Books, a division of
A & W Promotional Book Corp., New York, under
ISBN: 0-88365-082-7.

Printed in the United States of America

This book is affectionately dedicated
to the late ALFRED ADLER, whose teachings
have been our inspiration.

THE WILLARD AND MARGUERITE BEECHER FOUNDATION

The Willard and Marguerite Beecher Foundation is a non-profit corporation organized under the laws of Texas and operated exclusively for charitable, educational, and scientific purposes by furthering by clinical study, laboratory research, publication, and teaching the knowledge in the principles of the late Willard and Marguerite Beecher as exemplified in their books and writings.

All its directors serve gladly without remuneration. They have the one common bond that each was singly blessed by the teachings and writings of the Beechers. All are concerned that society continues to have available the important insights into human behavior and mature action which the late Beechers provided during their lifetime. The directors of the Foundation are:

The Foundation was formed with the knowledge and grateful approval of the Beechers. Prior to his death, Willard had given Bud Moshier his files of unpublished material along with permission to use them in any manner that was deemed valuable to others. Upon the establishment of the Foundation, Marguerite wrote Louise Raggio, "Wow! — I am overwhelmed by the stupendous job you have done. I send you my profound thanks. Just know that your efforts are deeply and intensely appreciated."

That intense appreciation is a two-way street. The Directors of the Foundation feel it is a privilege to be able to do something to repay the Beechers for their contribution to our individual and several lives.

The Willard and Marguerite Beecher Foundation Directors welcome your comment and/or inquiry. The address is 8400 Westchester, Suite 300, Dallas, Texas 75225.

ACKNOWLEDGMENT

We wish to thank David M. Engelhardt, M.D.,
for suggesting the title of this book.

The Authors

TABLE OF CONTENTS

ON A NOTE OF SANITY

The rising tide of juvenile delinquency and other difficulties with children of all ages has swelled to such proportions that social agencies, citizens' groups, and federal as well as state committees are being set up all over the United States to deal with the problem. We as adults must have failed somewhere. . . . The increasing prevalence of terror and violence constitutes a most serious and disturbing problem. Destruction of public and private property and of life itself is growing more frequent. The attitude of most of these children toward sex and the spending of money is like the slogan painted on some of their hot-rod cars: "Here we go! Four wheels and no brakes." Everyone, including the experts, is at a loss to understand what is happening. One thing is certain: we must straighten out this horrible condition.

Twenty years of experience with thousands of children and parents have convinced us that there is a way of life which can be satisfactory for both the youngsters and their harassed progenitors. We cannot say that it is a foolproof formula, but it does clear up the picture of general confusion and helplessness which has for too long dominated the scene. It makes for a happier, healthier relationship between children and their parents and the community. It points the way to further human progress without sacrificing the true dignity of the individual, be he child or adult.

This book deals with the common-sense factors that must

come into practice if our children are to grow into responsible members of our society. It is when they are young that the problems must be tackled. It is before they become delinquents and irresponsibles that we must do our job.

All difficulties of later life stem mainly from mistaken attitudes regarding human association. And these mistaken attitudes are acquired by the child in his earliest years, from life situations *we* present to him in his association with *us!*

This book is a plea for a plan—a prayer that something will be done, on a note of sanity, in the direction of constructive relationships. It is not intended to comfort either the proponents of the "hickory-stick school of thought" or the "child can do no wrong" contingent. It is not asking the impossible.

There is no greater gift an adult can give a child than a proper preparation for life. With such a gift in the beginning, the child is forever enriched. He will use it every day of his life as long as he lives and throughout every hour of the day. It is a gift that grows with use. With this gift he will enrich all those who come his way.

So, stop running! Dig in your heels. It's time to wrestle with the realities of the situation.

MARGUERITE AND WILLARD BEECHER

New York, June 1955

I

THE FAMILY PORTRAIT

1

PARENTS IN A QUANDARY

The morale of parents throughout this country has sunk to a notable low. They seem to be failing from exhaustion and uncertainty. Their hearts are weary. Their children are out of hand. And they do not know how to improve either the child's or their own situation. They search hopelessly, as if lost in a desert, for some oasis that will bring them relief and quench their thirst.

Time was when parents had their own authority about the rearing of children. In those days, children were supposed to be "seen and not heard." The fear of parents and of God was instilled in them. There was no back talk and no nonsense. The homes of yesteryear were adult-centered. Today we have the child-centered home. In it there is little peace and quiet, and certainly not much respect for, or fear of, authority. Today's comic-tragic home reveals the child is firmly and autocratically in command. Parents are barely tolerated around the house. Indeed, it is parents who are to "be seen and not heard." The highest law of today's home is the whim of the child. Parents are the ones who fear their children; and they have lost all courage to oppose them! In short, today the degradation of the parent, in too many instances, is practically complete. His role has become that of a beggar and a servant.

If we are to understand this reversal and the present low

morale of parents, we must place the situation in historical perspective. In early societies, the role of the child in relation to the adults was well defined and so much a matter of custom that no conscious thought was given it. In primitive societies, one does not find the child placed *before* the adult in rights and privileges. In such soceietes the child always had physical maturity as something for which to strive, and he gladly trained himself for the privileges he won when he was accepted as an adult. No one ever heard of a child-centered home or a child-centered school in a primitive society. Everyone understood that the child was to become a functioning member of the community as soon as his growth permitted, and he was properly trained to fulfill that role.

In Western civilization, when it became industrialized, the child began to be used for work in the factory and the mines. This led to a serious violation of his rights as a human being. Few children continued in school past the first eight grades. The majority were brought up in a harsh, repressive manner and were given no choice even in those areas where choice is rightfully their own. In the novels of Charles Dickens we are given a picture of the brutality with which parents treated their children. Even at the turn of this century, children were still exploited in sweatshops. The extent to which they were exploited economically depressed the wages of the adults who should have been doing the work. In time, it became evident that laws must be passed to free the child from some of the unfair burdens placed upon him and from those tasks that were harmful to his development.

Children fared no better in terms of self-determination in middle-class families. All the moralities and rigidities of the day were imposed on them, and in most families "Papa was boss," and what "Papa said was to be"—was!

The pendulum began to swing away from excessive pressure on children. And, as might have been expected, it swung to the opposite extreme. The early enthusiasts in child guidance believed that the "child could do no wrong" and that he should be left entirely to some inner instinct that would guide him surely to a perfect development, if only adults kept their hands off. At about the same time there came into being the progressive-education movement; its guiding rule was to remove every trace of outside authority from the child, in the hope that this would remedy all difficulties. Nothing should be imposed on the child, said these educators, lest his ego be damaged and his personality be ruined. In the "progressive" schools, children were allowed to do only what they wanted to do. The result was that bedlam reigned supreme in the classrooms. Second-graders often spent their time making applesauce and jelly. And by the fourth grade many of these children did not know even how to count or read. Some never learned these elementary skills at all, because of this hypnotic notion that neither parents nor teachers should demand anything of children.

These so-called child-centered-home and child-centered-school-curriculum concepts caught the imagination of parents to an amazing degree. Much of their support, of course, was a retroactive rebellion against the pressures placed upon them when they were children. As a result, they accepted a kind of tyranny and exploitation from their children such as they had never had from their own parents!

Moreover, the majority of parents accepted, whole hog, the dictum: "You must give your child love and security!" If giving a child love and security was of such paramount importance (and that's what the experts insisted), they determined to do it, regardless of the cost to themselves. What's more, they deliberately chose to believe—or, worse yet, they were deliberately led by some experts to believe—that to give a child love and security meant to give a child *everything*, even his OWN WAY AT ALL TIMES. The result of this uncritical acceptance by parents was that they brought up children who were insolent as well as demanding, and who knew no inner or outer controls. About the only genius their children seemed to develop was an amazing capacity to maintain the center of attention under any or all circumstances. Their children had plenty to *say* on all subjects but were prepared to *do* little, if anything, constructive.

The more parents gave, the more children expected. Parents found themselves on the horns of a dilemma. The result was that the parent had all the responsibility and the child had all the authority! The parent might reason, beg, nag, or bribe, but the child went his merry way, free as air, to follow his own whim of the moment and to do as he pleased. If that meant kicking Mama in the belly, clouting Dad over the head, demolishing the family car, or destroying the neighbor's picket fence—so what? Unfortunately, parents could not avoid their responsibilities and had to pick up the tab and pay the bill as they went along. Meanwhile, these children grew up physically (if not emotionally), but they were not the race of supermen envisioned by the child-guidance experts and educators. On the contrary, the more "uninhibited" children had been allowed to be, the less were they willing to accept any restraints when they should have been both willing and productive members of society. Work on a job or in their home was a discipline they could not endure. And, after marriage, they found that bringing up their own children was such a limitation of their "freedom" that they resented it and escaped in any way possible.

It has been apparent to many, and for a long time now, that this laissez-faire approach to child training was only the other side of the same old coin. The adult-centered home of yesteryear made parents the masters and children their slaves. The child-centered home of today has made parents the slaves and children the masters. There is no true cooperation in any master-slave relationship, and therefore no democracy. Neither the restrictive-authoritative technique of rearing children nor the newer "anything-goes" technique develops the genius within the individual, because neither trains him to be self-reliant.

Parents themselves are beginning to suspect that giving up their own rights and their own lives does not really prepare their children for a happy and constructive life. But the "give-the-child-everything" school of child guidance is far from being discredited. It is too well entrenched. Its proponents sit in high places and are very vocal. They still flood the press and the air waves with their viewpoint: that all that is wrong is that we aren't giving the child enough love. Many make policies in institutions that set the tone and direction of child guidance. Others may be opening their eyes and realizing that the King's New Clothes are invisible—but not these experts.

Meanwhile parents are deeply confused and dissatisfied. Long ago they gave up daring to trust their own good common sense, and no longer do they want to suffer the results of allowing their children to do exactly as they please. It is indeed fortunate that a dilemma has only two horns, or the situation might have become worse. This swing of the pendulum from severity to complete indulgence has demonstrated an important fact: a child brought up at either extreme is not properly prepared to face the world of reality. Neither prepares a child for becoming an adequate member of society. Children reared under arbitrary rules become either spineless automatons or bitter revolutionaries who waste their lives in conflict with those around them. But children who know no law higher than their own passing fancy become trapped by their own appetites. In either case, they are slaves. The former are enslaved by leaders on whom they depend to tell them what to do, and the latter are enslaved by the pawn-broker. Neither are capable of maintaining society on any decent basis. A lifetime of unhappiness may be avoided if the twig is bent so the tree will not incline in either of these mistaken directions.

2

HOW SHOULD THE TWIG BE BENT?

Anthropologists and sociologists who have studied primitive societies have made comparisons between the way the primitives handle their children and the way we handle ours. From these studies, one gets the impression that the primitive parents do what comes naturally in rearing their offspring.

In one culture, for instance, the mother may remain with her newborn infant for fourteen days and let it suckle at will. After that, she feeds the baby in the morning and goes into the fields to work all day long. The baby is cared for by some older person or by another child. When it wants to eat, the baby-sitter chews up food and puts it in the baby's mouth, until the mother returns at night. This is one of the less-indulged cultures. In others, children are indulged in every way, almost to the extent of being deified. One might wonder how such children, starting life from either of such extremes, could ever fit into the scheme of adult life.

This is not difficult to understand, on closer inspection. The pattern of tribal life is so simple that every child can understand it at an early age. His role is clearly defined for him, and he begins, with understanding, to imitate his elders in his play. The skills he must learn are mostly body skills and are not complex. They are not based on abstract intellectual concepts, therefore he doesn't run the risk of falling behind his

age group in his development. And, since the best teacher of a
child is another child, each one is stimulated to train himself
toward self-sufficiency in terms of tribal customs. His excitements lie in firsthand adventures rather than in the various
thrills of secondhand or psuedo excitements—television, comics, and the like—that distract our children from training for
adulthood. In such societies there are no exaggerated extremes
of high and low to confuse the child. The chieftain does not
live very much better than his subjects. And the whole group
works together for survival as a tribal unit rather than for individual supremacy. Parents do not experience the same kind
or degree of anxiety about their children as we do. It is therefore easier in every way for them to have a more relaxed attitude toward their children. They do not feel themselves
judged by the report card a child brings home from school.
Who ever heard of an I.Q.-dominated school in a primitive
society?

Primitive parents feel no need to nag their children endlessly to brush their teeth, keep their braces on, wash their
hands before eating, button up their overcoats, blow their
noses, hang up their clothes, wash behind their ears, practice
the piano, do their homework, prepare for examinations, bring
home good marks from school, and countless other admonitions that infuriate our children and make them frightened,
stubborn, and resentful. It is easier for children and parents to
enjoy each other in such simple cultures. Perhaps if we lived
in their simple environment, we could do it too. But this
explanation is certainly not meant to be interpreted as advo-
cating that we return to living in a mud hut.

What we are saying is that in our culture, adults' imposi-
tion on children of their own endless anxieties is one of the
most destructive forces brought to bear on a child. There is
much talk nowadays about children being exposed to "trau-
matic experiences," and numberless things are regarded as hav-

ing the power to traumatize or damage a child. But take any one of them as an example, and you will find a child somewhere who was exposed to the same kind of experience and was not damaged by it.

There is one important exception, however. *Every* child who is exposed to parental anxiety finds this a serious handicap to his development. The child is weak but regards his parents as omnipotent. If he sees that they are anxious and terrified by the problems of the outside world, he is doubly frightened, both by his own weakness and by theirs. He feels that his situation is probably hopeless. How can he hope to grow up and solve such problems if his strong parents find them insoluble? Parents may make any and all the mistakes in the book, and yet their children will survive with minimum damage if only the parents do not expose their own anxieties (infantilism) to the child. It is unfair to expect a child to develop courage when his parents broadcast their own fears in his hearing.

In primitive societies, where life is not so complex, there is no chance for parents to become so anxiety-ridden. Moreover, the role of the child is well defined and so much a matter of custom that no conscious thought need be given it. One does not find the child placed before the adult in rights and privileges. The child always has physical maturity and its privileges as something for which to strive. He gladly trains himself for the rights he wins when he is accepted as an adult. As a result, adulthood is no stranger to him, nor does he fear it. And he has a good perspective as to his own part in the melody of communal living and the survival needs of his tribe.

In our own civilization, which grows increasingly complex and technological, we have an even greater need for reconciling a child to the life he must lead as an adult. The very heart and hide of our education should be concerned with orienting children to live on a basis of mutually profitable human rela-

tionships. But it is in this very area of training for social behavior that we are failing our children so miserably. This
could not happen except that we have forgotten—or perhaps
never rightly understood—the basic principle on which the
survival of mankind depends. We have grown oblivious of
the obvious! If reminded of it, we are prone to shrug our
shoulders, because common sense is something we prefer to
ignore. The fact remains, however, that no shrug of the shoulders, no invention, no technological advances will ever relieve
us of the inexorable demands of productive community living.

From its beginning the human race has had to live on a
group basis. The fate of the individual has always been un-
alterably involved with the fate of his group. Man has always
been a part of a vast social context, and millions of years of
group living have proved that this is the best possible method
for survival.

Yet much of today's child guidance and counseling tends to
overlook this very fact. It is focused on explaining a child's
problems as though he were a one-ness thing and no one lived
within miles of him. It has tried to find the answer to the
child's difficulties by looking inside him. This has succeeded
only in compounding our confusion and intensifying our mis-
takenness. The course of disaster this has brought cannot be
altered until we give up looking at the individual as a thing-in-
himself rather than as part of a social fabric. Every human
problem is, in reality, a two-or-moreness thing. If we are to
understand any human problem, it can be only in relation to
the whole group of which a person is a part and in which he
moves. If a child is making problems in the home or the
school, it is senseless to look "inside" him, for the answer
to the problem lies in his way of relating himself to those
around him. And this grows out of their way of relating themselves to him. More than the child is involved in the child's

behavior! Wisdom demands that we look at our own roles in the failures of our children.

When we view mistrained and misguided children in their social context (that is, in their families, schools, neighborhood, and community), we find them in conflict and disrepute in all the areas of their lives. There is a fine mesh or whole web of symptoms and complications. Their parents are humiliated because the children are a burden, and disturbed because they don't know what to do about it. Their teachers are irritated for the same reason. Other children make or infer unpleasant comparisons. In short, the relationships of these so-called "problem" children are most unsatisfactory and devoid of useful compensations and human worth. If the problem goes far enough, the child may become a delinquent —a thief, a vandal, a drug addict, or even a murderer. In other words, the child has failed because he has not been trained to establish mutually profitable relationships with those around him. His activities are on the useless side of life. Because he operates in terms of "I," not "we," he threatens the security of others. Our schools, as time goes on, are labeling more and more of these children as mentally retarded or emotionally blocked.

Does this mean that the human race is spawning defective infants? The human race has survived thousands and thousands of years on this earth. Has something happened to the seed in recent years? Are today's primitive tribes afflicted by the same dry rot? Must we believe the gloomy predictions and poor prognoses made about these children? Are they really so defective? Or is it possible that there is something wrong with modern psychology? Is it, possibly, that our approach to, and training of, children has fallen down? Is it perhaps a judgment against ourselves rather than an indictment of the children?

It doesn't make sense—it makes nonsense to suppose that

the children of the human race have deteriorated so much in so short a time! It will be a Hallelujah Day when we see this problem as an invention of our minds. It is we who have erred, by somehow giving our children a wrong picture of themselves in relation to the world around them. It must be chalked up as our failure that we have not helped them to understand that they must cooperate as productive members of a team in order to coexist.

If we are to stem the rising tide of failing and delinquent children in our midst, it is a matter of urgency for us to retrain our own habits of thought about children and life. We have forgotten that we can only take out what we put in. No one is entitled to a free ride, and no mature person wants it. If our children are to feel secure, it is only justice to prepare them to understand and to accept the requirements and the responsibilities of adulthood.

3

JUSTICE IS SECURITY

We are indebted to a mother of five growing children for the title of this chapter. Recently she wrote us, "I think children, basically, want what is coming to them, good or bad, because *justice is security*. There are times when my feet do hurt, too much milk goes on the floor, the washing machine breaks down—and my temper gets short. But I feel it is all part of a child's education. When I line my five children up at night and say, 'For Pete's sake, go to bed. I am tired. I am hungry. I am sick of looking at kids. If you aren't out of sight in two minutes flat, I'll grind you up into hamburgers!'—each one of the five looks sympathetic. Not one of them takes this personally, and each one thinks to himself, 'It's a dirty shame how those other four kids wear Mama out. They ought to be murdered.' Since the others sometimes get in their hair, it is only reasonable for each of them to assume that I am human, too. It is all very humanizing."

This is a human mother who treats her children humanly. Since childhood is only the training period for future life, a home should always be a small segment of the outside world. Far too many homes today, however, are run as if they were hothouses. Children reared in such hothouses feel chilled when they go into the outside world. As a result, they resent the treatment they get outside and they resist moving toward independence. They much prefer to remain in the warmth of their homes, where every whim is catered to and where all is given them in exchange for nothing more than their cries and their petulance.

To pamper is not to give love. Pampering is a malignant poison. When a doctor recommends a drug, he knows whether it is—or is not—dangerous to people, and he adjusts the dosage accordingly. If we tell the average person to "give love," we may be recommending poison unawares. This is possible because the word "love" is habitually used to cover opposite meanings. One kind of love enriches all around it, and the other kills all it touches. It is our tragedy that we use the same word for such dissimilar attitudes.

Unfortunately, perhaps its most common meaning is to devour, possess, hold on to, or otherwise remove from circulation in order to enhance oneself. Frequently we hear a person say, for example, "I love ice cream." This means that the person loses no chance to obtain some. He devours it. There is an empty plate left when he has finished. He has enriched himself.

This is an infantile expression of love. In the beginning of life, the infant is mostly a consumer of goods and knows nothing of the satisfactions to be had from producing or creating. The child "loves" the parents, who *give* him food, pleasure, comfort, or indulgence. He rejects those people and things that deny or limit his appetite to consume what pleases him. Very often a child may bypass his parents and turn to his grandparents or some other indulgent relative because that person gives more generously to him than his parents have.

A child has not developed to the point where he can create satisfactions for himself and by himself. His appetites must be largely satisfied from outside himself during his earliest years. His physical and psychic growth depend on his ingesting vast quantities of food and stimuli from those around him. It is not strange, then, that he should turn to, and try to possess, those who supply the things he wants and needs. Nor is it surprising if he resents parents who deny him second helpings of his favorite food, and turns his "love" to Grandma, who lets him have all he wants. In short, his "love" includes Grandma not because she is Grandma but because she represents less limitation of his desires.

Nothing in this concept of love, as manifested by a child, represents a protective, cherishing desire. In its expression there is no evidence of a desire to enrich, enhance, amplify, fertilize, germinate, create, produce, or develop either people or situations. Nature intended the child to be a consumer of goods and services in the beginning. But nature also demands that as he grows, he develop a love of "giving out" that is at least as strong as his desire to "take in." If he is to live healthily and happily he must learn the joy of creation and of using his inherent powers to accomplish something. He cannot find fulfillment if he is concerned only with what he can get from those around him.

The word "love" can mean, then, either *destructive dependence* or *constructive independence*. And, according to the emotional maturity of the individual who uses it, it can mean either giving out or taking in. The jealous child or the jealous mate "loves" at the infantile level of engulfment and possession. As long as he is able to use, to occupy, or to consume the loved object, without any limit to his appetite, he is satisfied. This type of love, however, turns to fury at any denial or even at the threat of denial or limitation. Many a jealous husband has killed his wife, and when asked why, has said that he loved her so much he could not bear to see anyone else have her. Such individuals have not developed past the devouring, nutritive stage of infancy.

It is a bitter fact that competition and rivalry set individuals at cross-purposes to one another. This does not predispose them to love, in the mature sense of the word. If a person loves his children or his partner or his friends, in a mature sense, he will love them in a way that will *free* them to develop their inner powers toward their own fulfillment. He will do it even though such development causes them to outgrow and outdistance him in the process of their maturing. Unfortunately, more people strive to bind their mates, friends, or children to them than to help them develop to their fullest, regardless of the path they may take to their future.

It is easy to see, then, why it is not enough to advise parents to "love their children," without knowing what level of love these parents are capable of giving. For example, many parents—without even being aware of it—regard their children as articles of personal adornment. They want their children to reflect credit on them and make them proud. This is a human desire. However, too many parents develop bitter resentments if their child lets them down in the eyes of those around them. If their child does not get "straight A's" on his report card, and the neighbor's child does, they often so humiliate their offspring with comparisons and scoldings that the child becomes discouraged and unwilling to try. Or if a father is a sports fan and his son likes poetry, the son is often made to feel ashamed of his "weakness" and he then becomes resentful of the father. There was a story in the newspapers, not so long ago, about a college boy who gave his parents cyanide because they had humiliated him continuously for his interest in aesthetic things. They were well-to-do parents and had loved their son so much, in their mistaken way, that they had given him everything—except a chance to be himself, with honor. Instead of guiding him to becoming a grownup, they smothered him into becoming a criminal!

Then there are many parents who themselves come from poor families and who were forced to become wage earners at an early age to help the family survive. As a result, they grew up to be hard workers with good jobs. However, resenting their beginnings and envying those who had easier childhoods, they frequently hit back at life by giving their own children the kind of pampering they imagine they would have chosen for themselves. So they unwittingly rear their children to believe that all is free for the asking. When they find their children growing up to be helpless, irritating people, they are hurt. They come to resent having to give endlessly of themselves and of their money. More than that, they come eventually to resent their selfish children.

One such father made this very mistake. He said, "I was born in the slums. My folks were poor. I felt deprived throughout my childhood. I vowed that when I grew up I would work hard and make a lot of money so that my children would not experience what I did." And he kept his vow. He had two children, a girl and a boy. Both were pampered, especially the boy, who was the younger. He was pampered not only by his father but also by his mother and his sister, who was so much older that she was essentially a "third" parent. They all waited on him and catered to him. They did for him all the things that he should have been doing for himself. They even thought for him and did his schoolwork for him. He had only to whine to get anything he wanted. By the time he was nine, he was failing in school and in other life areas. He did not make friends. He had no hobbies. He completely lacked initiative. He was like a lump of putty. As a result of the school's insistence, guidance help was sought by the father. In the process of re-education, the father confided with tears in his eyes, "You know, I thought that by giving my son everything, I was giving him love. Now I see the mistake. My son has only 'larceny in his heart'!"

Indulging a child is certainly not the same as loving a child. There can never be a time when such mistaken love will be a proper preparation for the child's adult life. The preceding example should not be misunderstood. We do not mean one must begin life in poverty and deprivation in order to become strong. Our strength lies in the use we make of our gifts and possessions. A person may have great wealth, beauty, and education but use them for no productive purpose. Another person, less fortunate and gifted, may use his talents fully and become a great social asset who improves the lot of himself and others. In short, life's race is not so much to the swift as to those who use their powers toward social goals.

It makes no difference whether one wants only to ride the merry-go-round at Coney Island or tour the country in his own Cadillac—someone has to pay for it! Everything and every service in the outside world has a price tag on it. The rule of payment for value received is much more than a cold, hard, unpleasant pill to force down the throats of unwilling children. It is a law of life that applies to all of us. Those who go through life trying always to *get*, without giving in return, lead bitter and discontented lives. They are parasites. They beg their way through life, rather than pay their way. No child who is brought up to believe "he's got it coming to him," no matter what, can possibly become a useful, well-adjusted adult. The human way of life is the community way of life, and community living is made possible only by keeping a fine balance between the law of mutual give and take.

A child must learn this fact early in his life, lest he be shocked or weakened when it comes time for him to go out on his own into the market place which is the outside world. If he does not learn it, he may be emotionally maimed for the rest of his life. He will not be able to meet the demands, emotional as well as material, that will be made upon him in this complex world of ours. The extent to which parents may fail their children in this respect was described by Edward Strecker, an Army psychiatrist, in his book, *Their Mothers' Sons*. He described the vast numbers of emotionally maimed boys who were found unfit for service in the United States Army during the last war. He states that there were 1,825,000. rejected right at the start for this very reason, to say nothing of the thousands who had to be discharged after enlistment, or the thousands who tried to evade the draft. He makes it unmistakably clear that these boys were "loved" by their parents in the most possessive way. As a result, they were unfit to stand on their own feet in their country's emergency—and only inadequately in civil life.

Possessive love damages the giver as well as the victim. A parent who wants to possess a child dares not deny him anything, even though it is for the child's eventual good, for fear of losing his approval. Parents who are so pathetically dependent on the moment-to-moment approval of a child that they cannot deny him anything are to be pitied. This is deplorable, because a child is maimed for life if his only bench mark is "I want."

A child who has been reared on a pampering basis is no more acquainted with love than a child who has been hated. In both cases the child grows up without ever knowing what being loved means. Love rightly expressed is the desire to see something outside oneself grow into its own fruition. A wise parent knows he will not always be around to help his child. He expresses true love when he does not stand in the way of the child's fulfillment and when he trains the child to help himself.

The pendulum that swung from an earlier era of severity to the more recent era of indulgence must swing again. There is nowhere for the pendulum to swing but into the middle, and the time is now—for justice is security.

4

IT'S HIGH TIME FOR A CHANGE

Now is the time to change our attitudes about the rearing of children. We must get off the horns of the dilemma on which we have been caught so long. We need a new look. We must seek new means to the end of preparing our children more properly for the society in which they will live as adults and to which they will be expected to make a useful contribution.

Parents need to give up the notion that they should protect their children in the safe harbor of a home that is completely unlike the stormy seas of life upon which their children must one day sail. To do this, parents must surrender the philosophy of being a child's "keeper." A child is not theirs to "have and to hold forever and a day"! A child is a *transient* who comes into the lives of parents for a brief period. He stays only a few years before he must be on his way to his own fulfillment. Mothers and fathers should live with each child so that they are happy to greet the child when he comes to them and happy to see him go when the time comes for going. Their own relationship as man and wife should not be weakened in the process of bringing up their children, for they must spend the rest of their lives together after the children have left home.

Parents have greater responsibilities than children and must, therefore, have the final authority about the home, family expenditures, and similar things, just as they must have final authority on matters concerning health. They should never allow the child's appetites to rule them, as these appetites rule the child. Children should never be allowed to disrupt their parents' lives or their development as people. Such a situation cannot possibly be right for society, for the parents, or for the children.

Children should be trained for independence. If they are not made independent, they will behave throughout their days as emotional cripples. If they are allowed to remain dependent, the parents are so occupied with trying to help these leaning children, that they lose sight of each other. If children are badly pampered and do not learn to be self-sufficient, then they are never free of their parents, nor are their parents free of them. Even though they may marry, they bring their burdens as well as their own offspring back to their parents. Under such circumstances, mothers and fathers remain burdened with insoluble problems and worries to the end of their days, and children never grow into happy maturity.

Parents have to learn to be loyal to each other and to stand together. Their children should always take their proper places in the family life. Far too often a child or children take first place in the life of a mother, and her husband is pushed aside. In such cases the parents become emotionally estranged and do not act in unison toward the child. It does not take long for the child to discover this fact. Then he learns how to play one parent against the other—to burn the candle at both ends—and in so doing, he can hold the dominant position. Thus the deciding vote is in the child's hands at all times. Countless divorces arise from this kind of situation. The child, unfortunately, loses out on all fronts. His parents are miserable and he becomes miserable, too.

When, for instance, a choice must be made by parents as to whether they should have a much-needed vacation together or whether their children should have a television set, the parents should *always favor themselves.* Parents need to keep themselves physically and emotionally fit so they can meet the countless responsibilities they must face. And when parents treat themselves with respect, children learn to respect them as people for the simple reason that they, as parents, respect *themselves!* If parents always serve their children first at the table and in every other life situation, the children build up an attitude of superiority and feel that they should always come first in all matters. This false sense of importance leads them to feel that their parents are not worthy of consideration except as servants to them. And their tendency will be to think of all other people as their servants.

Parents who always consider themselves as well as their children *do not find their children to be a burden to them,* and they can enjoy their families. The children love and respect their parents, too, and learn to value them as the parents value themselves. In families where parents always provide first for their children and take too little for themselves, the children do not learn to value what is given them, and certainly do not value the parents who provide the gifts. Nor do such children learn to value the worth of other people. The outcome of being badly spoiled and pampered is that such children all too commonly end up feeling "smothered" and having a sort of hatred for their parents. They grow up to become maladjusted adults.

This does not mean that parents should never give their children gifts. But they should be sure that what is given will be used by the child for his development and pleasure. Often, for example, children tease for music lessons, not because they really want them but only because some other child they know is taking piano lessons. Many parents are easily deluded into believing the child wants to learn to play the piano, when all he wants is to "get as much." After a few lessons, such children refuse to practice. Arguments and resentments precede and follow each lesson. The parent is angry and tense. So is the child. And so is the piano teacher. Instead of pursuing such a nonsensical course, the privilege of piano lessons should be withdrawn at once, until the child is ready to use it justly.

A child should be given every opportunity to follow his own genius, but neither the parents nor the home should be sacrificed to enable him to do so. If a child refuses to take the proper responsibility for a privilege given him, he should not have it until he is willing to value it. This point is very difficult for the majority of parents today to accept. The propaganda about giving a child everything, lest his personality be ruined, is now so ingrained in parents that it is hard for them to conceive of denying a child anything. They are not used to thinking of training a child on a "pay-as-you-go" basis, even though they themselves are aware that this is the very basis and ethic of social life.

They do not comprehend that to allow a child to believe that life is a "something-for-nothing" business is to sponsor his living in infantile fantasy. They admit and even complain that their children's minds are only on play. They confess that any suggestion on their part that their children contribute something useful to the well-being and well-running of the household is greeted with a storm of protest. But in most cases these selfsame parents are so intimidated that they dare not demand that their children do something useful first and play later. If they do, the emotional storm blots out their words. This succeeds in causing them to capitulate. By these means their children merrily continue to rule the household with cries, complaints, untidyness, dawdling, and similar techniques!

One such girl of eight years managed to dominate and control her mother, father, and an older sister. She was more clever, in getting her own way, than the three of them put together. She could outtalk and outargue all of them. She could trap them into centering attention upon her by such simple expedients as malingering, restlessness, insubordination, jeering, yells, fears, and what not. She was a female Hitler! Both at home and at school she created distractions to force others to stop whatever they were doing and look after her needs. Wherever she went she managed to keep everybody occupied with her. None of this cost her a single thing, and she had the pure pleasure of laughing at everyone when she proved her will stronger than theirs. Though she "made like a ruler," she suffered from persisting infantilism, since she demanded more attention than a newborn baby, which at least sleeps part of the time! Her parents and teachers were unaware of the extent to which their catering and pampering had crippled this child.

Children of this type, if the course of their infantilism is not halted, will be emotionally maimed throughout their days. They will expect people outside the home to make concessions and to pamper them as their parents have done. Alfred Adler said: "Education accompanied by too much tenderness is as pernicious as education which proceeds without it; a pampered child, as much as a hated child, labors under the greatest difficulties." Parents and children have to learn to live together on a "live-and-let-live" basis. It is time to agree that neither the child nor the adult should have complete ascendency—that one should not completely dominate the other.

The whole essence and preservation of a democratic way of life lies in the direction of this new look: a "let's-take-turns" doctrine rather than one of "me first, you second." It is not so difficult to work out such a program for the training of our children. We can arrive at it easily by considering how our automobile traffic problem was solved: by the simple formula, "You let me pass this time and I will let you pass next." All relationships within a family should be made on such a basis and kept mutually profitable for both parents and children. Parents, then, have only to learn that they, **as** well as their children, have rights!

5

PARENTS HAVE RIGHTS, TOO

The trend toward considering the child first and foremost has been an alarmingly effective "party line." It has so seriously entrapped parents that they fear to institute a program of "equal rights" when it is first suggested. To try to get parents today to begin to think of asserting their rights as parents is almost like shouting in the desert. They will cling steadfastly to the notion that a child has more rights than they have, even in those areas where the child is neither old enough nor experienced enough to have understanding. Yet they complain bitterly, meanwhile, about their so-called "problem children."

Parents' complaints offer much material that indicates the extent to which they have lost their rights. Take something simple like the telephone. Many parents do not feel free, if one of their children gets on the phone and talks for hours, to stop the conversation or to interrupt it even for a short time. But if you ask them who it is that pays the freight, they will grin sheepishly. Nevertheless, they continue to argue that the child has more rights to the house than they have, even though, as a result of such nonsense, they have experienced all too painfully the arrogance and tyranny of their children. Their children treat them exactly as if they were lackeys!

This is the way Arthur treated his parents. By the age of fourteen he had a viselike grip on his parents. They were without rights and were treated as flunkies by their son. On three different occasions, when Arthur was younger, the school had urged them to seek guidance. They had done so, but each time they had been advised, in essence, that they must stop nagging their son, lest he feel insecure and unloved! And so Arthur grew up to be a truant, a spendthrift, and an arrogant tyrant. He would strike his father if refused permission to go out with his gang. If his folks bought something they needed for the home, he would order them to return it and would say, "You do not need that. Give me the money." If his mother tried to carry on a telephone conversation, he would yank the telephone out of her hands. He would physically force his mother into a corner to make her obey. If he sat right next to the kitchen sink, he would yell to his mother in the next room to come draw a glass of water for him. He forced her to serve his meals on a tray in his room, to shut his door, to put on his socks, to lace his shoes, to go out and buy him a comic book or to "flip papers" so that he could decide whether he would or would not go to school or keep an appointment at the doctor's! Although he was in junior high school, he would make his parents read to him while he played with a nursery game of toy wagons!

Parents do not enjoy such treatment from a child. No one likes to be degraded to the position in which Arthur's parents found themselves. But they had gradually lost their authority and their rights because they had given in to his demands over the years prior to adolescence. Now Arthur was so strong that they feared physical violence if they refused to submit to his whims. Because they felt hopeless of regaining their proper place in Arthur's life, they preferred not to hear any suggestions that would put them on the firing line.

Parents would not go astray in the first place if they reflected just a little about the whole question of "rights." A parent is an adult, but being an adult does not give him the right to live in a house unless he pays for it. He has no right to a car unless he pays for it. He may not drive it unless he takes full responsibility of operating within the traffic code. He may not have clothes, food, services, or other things provided from the outside unless he pays for them. In short, rights are in *direct ratio to the amount of responsibility* one is willing to take.

Community life and social life become impossible if and when authority is separated from responsibility. The adult who acts on his own authority, without taking commensurate responsibility, is quickly locked up in a mental institution or jail. Society allows us to move only as long as we remain responsible for our movements. And for every right there is an equivalent responsibility.

By the same token, some adults have greater responsibility than others. *To them must be given an equal amount of authority.* We could not demand that anyone be President of the United States of America unless we gave him more authority than an average man. We give him special authority because we have given him special responsibilities.

It is an obvious fact that the responsibilities of parents are far greater than those of children. Parents are responsible to each other, to their children, to the grocer, the butcher, to the school, and to the state, to name only a few. It is the parent who is punished if anything goes wrong. Parents are not free to do as they please. In bringing up their children, they must meet certain minimum demands of the community. If they fail, they are penalized and their children are taken from them to be given to others who *will* take the responsibility.

To allow a child to assume that his rights are of paramount importance is to seriously and dangerously mistrain him for community life. He should be trained from the beginning to know that an individual's rights are no greater than his responsibility in any situation. For example, parents pay for the telephone. If they allow a child to use it, that is a *privilege* they give him. It is not a *right*. The privilege should be revoked if the child does not take proper responsibility. Piano lessons are a privilege, too, to be earned by the child when he takes his lessons seriously and works at them. He must learn to understand that he is not entitled to make demands until he is in a position to give a fair exchange. It is in just such simple ways that a child is best trained for living in our society.

Children take for granted the shelter, clothes, education, and all else that parents provide for them. They often complain bitterly because what they get is not as good as what some neighbor's child has. They feel that they have a right to as big an allowance, a right to stay up as late, to have a television set, to go on trips, and to do whatever their more fortunate neighbors do. They feel bitter if their parents dare to refuse them. They would not have such nonsensical ideas if their parents had trained them from the start that rights and responsibilities are tied together in this world. There will never be a time when the train engineer on duty has the "right" to sit in the club car and drink with the passengers! He has the responsibility for the lives of all of them, and he must watch the track. Thus it is with parents and children. Each must know the reality of the situation, and each must observe it in relation to the others.

Parents who have demanding, tyrannical, and arrogant children should have suspected that they were being misled by the child-guidance experts and that they were making serious mistakes in the rearing of their children. They should have suspected that instead of teaching their children to grow up, they were training them to remain infants. At any rate, the fact remains that today they do not understand how their best intentions and all their good efforts could have brought such results. The better their intentions, the more difficult it is for them to accept their failures. Their outraged sense of justice leads them to put the blame on the child, on his inheritance, on some early illness, on the school, on anything that cannot be attributed to them. They are deeply angry, and the fact is that they really do not know what to blame. In desperation they try to cover up the child's deficiencies by finding some scapegoat.

This feeling of anger (guilt) often prevents parents from facing the situation for what it is, in the effort to begin a reorientation of all concerned. But all that is needed is a reappraisal of the way in which the family lives together. Parents must be helped to make the *human situation humanly straight*. One of the first things they must do is to face up to the fact that they have created a situation in which their children can and do exploit them, and that this exploitation is part of the whole problem of their "problem" children. They must see that they have allowed themselves to be degraded and put upon when there is no need for it.

If the human situation is to be made humanly straight, parents must win back their own independence *at an action level* and refrain from being used only as conveniences. It does not take too long, after parents gain insight, to alter mistaken family relationships and for the parents to get back a large area of the independence they have lost to their children.

When parents begin to regain their self-respect, the most amazing changes begin to take place in their children. Phrases such as "I want" and "you must give me" gradually disappear. Children start to help themselves when no one helps them. They begin to earn their allowance when they discover that they will not get it if they have done no useful work or made no contribution to the well-being of the home. They learn to take care of their clothes if all extra clothing is removed when it is not properly valued. Children are very intelligent people. Their intelligence should never be underestimated. They know exactly on what side their bread is buttered! *They live with us exactly as we live with them.* And when we change our way of living with them, they quickly respond and change their way of living with us.

When parents stop being beggars, children cannot withhold. The degraded parent of a spoiled child must beg, scold, and plead, but he still ends up getting nothing from the child. Parents who have stopped begging and stopped "giving for nothing" soon find themselves in a new situation as far as their children are concerned. The children quickly learn that they must come to the parents with a *result in hand* in order to win advantages in the family. Then family life becomes rewarding for both parents and children. There is some peace and freedom in the home, and the promise of growth and fun together. This is the way it should be. In a home, friendship rather than tyranny should reign.

The parent who seeks a solution to his child's problem will not find it because to expect a child to change when he is sitting on the throne of authority is to expect too much. The day parents begin to work on their own problems, the child can only improve. We cannot control others, but we can control the way we relate to others. Any parent can find the courage to change his own behavior. Any parent who is willing to take this step toward self-rehabilitation is on the proper path. He must set the pace and direction of his own movement toward equality. Equality begets equality. When a parent is able to regard himself as a person in his own right, no child can exploit him further.

An analogy about a man and his dog may help to clarify what happens when a person has his own authority—or hasn't. First let us consider a man who takes a walk and allows his dog to accompany him. The man decides to walk a mile and return. As he goes along, the dog runs here and there, sometimes ahead, sometimes behind. He chases a cat or stops to romp with another dog. But the man continues on his own independent journey and returns, for he is operating on his own authority. When he gets home, the dog is *with him*. In this instance, it is the dog's job to keep abreast of the man. Now let us consider a dog-centered world, with a man who takes a walk with his dog. Wherever the dog goes, the man feels compelled to follow. The dog goes at random across country and forbidden territory. His only objective is to go where he pleases, and he is in no hurry to return. Whether they return at all is no concern of the dog's!

By the same token, parents who set the limits and objectives of the family as a whole, and do not lose sight of their own objectives, set a pace. Their children will not be far behind them. But parents who let the whims of children set the pace and direction do not find their way out of the wilderness in which they wander. Their children show little if any concern. Why should they? They are in the driver's seat. Yet these tyrannical children are not happy, for they know not where the limits are—if any. They are children in "search of limits"!

6

CHILDREN IN SEARCH OF LIMITS

A whole generation or more of parents have been led to believe that there is something wrong or evil about indoctrination and the exercise of any authority over children. The folly of this campaign now greets us in newspaper headlines and screeches at us from the air waves. We are now confronted with a Pandora's box of evils—evils much worse than the one parents were supposed to be avoiding! Where is it to end:—the rising incidence of illiteracy, the school failures, the juvenile vandalism, sex orgies, dope addiction? What shall we do to prevent an increase in this army of children in search of limits?

Certainly one can agree that a child should not be brought up under a discipline that permits him no choice and no self-expression. As long as a child is willing to live on the useful side of life, he should be given as much free choice as his years warrant. It is no great matter if a child does not wash his hands as often as his parents wash theirs. Parents should endure a certain amount of dirt on their children at times. But if a child puts his dirty hands on the walls and spoils the wallpaper that his parents have worked so hard to buy, then he has gone beyond his personal rights and should be stopped. The child who is a vandal in his home may carry his vandalism out of the home and become a problem for the whole community. There is a very narrow line between "mine" and "thine," but a child should learn to recognize it as early in life as possible. Others outside the home will not indulge him if he spoils their property, nor will they tolerate his usurping their rights. If he learns in the home to observe the line between what belongs to him and what belongs to his parents or his brothers and sisters, he will find it easy to live in the outside world. And parents will find it easy to live with him.

Parents must learn that they cannot be charged with full responsibility for the development of children unless they have commensurate authority. Parents must recognize that any school of child guidance that counsels them always to allow children to have their own way cannot possibly be right. For the attitudes and behavior that are learned in the early years of a child's life become the pattern on which the rest of his life is built.

Maturity includes the recognition that we have to pay for what we receive. Life demands that we give as good as we get. Every type of immaturity has at its core the desire to secure personal advantage without giving anything in return. Parents who are afraid to "deny" children undeserved privileges are training them to fail in life. The child who is the center of attention at home will expect such special privileges when he goes outside the home. He will resent sharing attention with others and will make disturbances calculated to draw attention to himself. He will be a burden to others, not a help. Of such stuff is neurosis made!

At birth the child is the most dominant person in the world. He is completely helpless. Because of this, we must serve him in every way. He appears to know no mercy and not to care whether or not we are tired. His cry is our command, and we must give him what he needs. Our own wishes must be put aside for his.

However, society could not continue if this condition were allowed to persist indefinitely. From the day of birth we must begin to free ourselves of the child's dependency. After a few months the baby does not need the nighttime feedings, and in due time he fits his hunger into our plan of eating only three times a day. Thus some of his "tyranny" over us is diminished. When he learns to control elimination, to walk, talk, dress, and to do similar things, he is freeing us further from our slavery to him. Our whole objective as educators of the child should be to *regain our freedom* from him so that he may *gain his freedom* from us.

If adults fail to free themselves from the infantile demands of children, these children grow up to become jealous, competitive individuals. In the beginning, children must have parents in order to survive at all. If parents start at the birth of a child (at least in their own minds) to free themselves from his unnecessary demands, and train him to help himself as he grows physically and mentally, he learns to enjoy doing things for himself and grows more healthily. The satisfaction he derives from his increasing freedom stimulates him to greater efforts in the direction of self-sufficiency. He should turn to the parents only for those things that are really beyond his immediate powers. If a parent is consistently too helpful to a child, the child does not discover and develop his own ability to help himself. He expects the parent to spoon the food into his mouth, cut up his meat, bathe him, and otherwise look after him. Should the parent, at a later time, choose to withdraw such unnatural and now unwarranted support, the child becomes resentful and feels insecure. He is not prepared to function alone in such situations. He usually sets up a fuss that drags the now unwilling parent back into his service. Neither child nor parent feels happy in such situations.

What is so evil about indoctrination for self-reliance? Why

shouldn't we indoctrinate children to be self-sufficient and productive? The outside world demands only two things: that we maintain ourselves and not burden others. It should not be either evil or difficult to train our children in these two principles. Since these are the basic material for social living, we should make them a goal of our educational efforts with children. We should regard the education of children as incomplete if there are notable defects in these areas.

The child who is not trained for self-reliance will not be interested in, and can never hope to unfold, his own potentialities—not until or unless he learns on his own to help himself and not be a burden on those around him. To lean on others without compensating them is to exploit their strength. No society built on sheer exploitation can persist. A child who only leans on others can never go farther than others are willing to carry him. Even the foolish parent eventually gets fed up with the demanding child.

Fellow feeling is the other element that must be developed in a child. None of us can retire to a private world. If we are to survive at all as human beings, we must share this earth together in a scheme of mutuality. Since no man can live alone, we have to learn to think in terms of "We." The other fellow will always be with us; and together we can do much more than we could do separately. This we should be trained to understand and to accept in our early years. The tasks of life depend on teamwork. Teamwork, in turn, depends on each doing his own job completely.

When fellow feeling is low or absent, a relationship disintegrates rapidly. No relationship can persist for long if it is lacking in mutual advantage. Human relationships are not notably different from business relationships. No merchant could remain in business if he continuously gave too much or too little to his customers. If he were to give too much—as does the average parent today—he would not be able to replace his stocks because of his policy of selling below cost price. He would eventually be bankrupt. Likewise, if he demanded too much he would lose his customers. The world of the home is not immune to the law of compensation that operates in the outside world. One must eventually exchange goods for goods, if bankruptcy is to be avoided.

The foolish parent who tries to protect a child from all hardships abrogates the law of mutual advantage. When the parent tries to smooth out and relieve all social and school difficulties, the child does not learn to handle such situations himself. More than that, the child anticipates that everything will be done for him in the future as in the past. He hopes to continue endlessly "living as a worm in an apple," with only the soft, sweep pulp to gnaw. (This might be good work if you could get it!)

The manner in which we live with children is what teaches them these basic facts of life—not what we tell them. Children do not learn from our words, for "telling" is not training. For example, we often hear a parent today droning, "I have told him a hundred times" (to do this or that). Such a parent should know that if the child hasn't learned by a hundred tellings, he won't learn by a hundred and one! But worse yet, this complaint reveals the parent's irresponsibility. It signifies that this parent has failed to train the child to understand that living also means to be a help.

Bill's mother trained him to understand that he must be a help. When she needed help with some chore or wanted an errand run, she did not hesitate to call on Bill. It did not occur to Bill not to be a help until a new boy moved into the neighborhood. Bill learned to his amazement that his new friend wouldn't help his mother or run an errand unless he was paid first! So the next time Bill's mother asked him to run an errand he said, "I will if you pay me." With guileless sweetness his mother replied smilingly, "Well, now, I'll pay you when you pay me." "Pay you for what?" Bill asked. His mother answered wryly, "When you pay me for making your meals, washing, ironing, and mending your clothes, for keeping your room clean, I'll pay you for running errands." Bill ran the errand and, while running it, he mulled over the many things his mother did for which he should rightly pay her. Bill's mother had a master plan. It read: "Train this boy to pay his way in life."

Too often, the mother of today gives all and asks nothing. She thus teaches her children to expect everything and to give NOTHING in return. When her children are old enough to run errands, they feel unjustly abused if she requests them to do so. She has taught them that it pays to remain a baby! They see no profit in being useful by helping her, themselves, or anyone. No one is trained for maturity in this fashion.

Training for maturity requires a plan. This plan should incorporate allowing a child to have his little problems and to experience his own limitations, according to his age. Without such a plan, the child has no incentive to grow up or to learn to solve his own problems. Children need not *like* to run errands. But they do need to understand that in the give-and-take of life they have to do their share of giving, and they have to accept their share of difficulties. Small difficulties in early life teach us and prepare us so that later on in life, when larger issues confront us, the spirit is not crushed. Life is not a bowl of pitted cherries, and we must not falsify it to children. The parent who cannot let a child experience reasonable frustrations and learn to surmount them stands in the way of the child's proper development. Such a parent builds a wobbly future for a child.

7

PARENTS NEED A MASTER PLAN

When a carpenter starts to build a house he has a master plan. Parents should have a master plan, otherwise each member of the family operates according to his own blueprint. If each member of a family has his own blueprint, it is much the same as if a number of individuals decided to build a house and each had his own design in his head. In such a situation, all that would be needed to compound the confusion would be for each to speak a different language. Only a tower of Babel can be built in a family where there is no master plan-for-all.

In homes where parents do not have control, a tower of Babel is essentially what happens. It is up to the parents to draw the plan by which they and the children shall live together. The children should make suggestions, to be sure, but it is for the parents to make the final decisions as to how the human situation is to be kept humanly straight. Each member of the family must know his responsibilities to every other member and to the total situation. The parents know the size of the family income and the needs of the family. They know the space needs of each member and the total available space. Since crowding has become an increasingly important factor in our lives, each must content himself with less and use the common spaces with more reserve. There is an old saying that "many patient sheep can lie down in one stall." But if even one is impatient, the whole group is thrown into an uproar and all are trampled.

In homes where there is no master plan there is much trampling about. Parents soon find that they have lost control of their homes and that their children have developed strong rivalries. In these homes one finds each child has his own plan as to how things should be done and has his own private idea of what is his right in any given situation. As a result, petty grievances begin to accumulate and everyone—parents and children alike—becomes irritable and irritating. An all too common pattern of confusion and aggravation begins to emerge.

We might illustrate by describing one such home where bedlam reigned. There were two adolescent daughters who were of an age to get telephone calls from boys. If one received a call, she would hang on to the telephone for three quarters of an hour while the other made frantic cries that she would not get her calls. But when she did get on the telephone, she did exactly the same thing. Their parents had no chance whatsoever to use the phone during the evening. No matter that Father expected an important business call that would consummate a deal, or that Mother, as president of the PTA, had necessary calls to make. All they were supposed to do was pay for the telephone bills!

Bitter fights between the daughters was the benchmark of this home. Its peace was endlessly disturbed. There were two bathrooms in the apartment, one with more mirrors and better equipment. The girls insisted on using the well-mirrored bathroom. Occasionally the father managed to get into this bathroom to shave. Whenever he did, his daughters pounded on the door. Although he did not surrender it each time they pounded, he had no peace, for his daughters kept pounding, sputtering, and scolding through the door as long as he remained in the bathroom.

It was not only the bathroom and the telephone that were matters of dispute. Although each girl had her own room, the sisters constantly intruded on each other, uninvited. They raided each other's wardrobes without permission and even wore their mother's clothes. Each daughter behaved as though she owned everything in the house and as though the other members of the family were hostile bandits intent on stealing what belonged to her! Each felt damaged when she didn't get her own way or when she could not operate according to her own private blueprint. As for the parents, they were always treated as if they were interlopers or unwelcome guests in the home. These girls were so ill-mannered and argumentative at mealtimes that their parents not only could not digest their meals properly but had ceased, long since, to invite guests to share a meal with them. Mother could not entertain her bridge club or carry on a conversation with her own friends in any comfort because her daughters' arguments, screams, and physical combats always disturbed such social affairs. Father could not relax on Sunday and read his newspapers for the same reason.

It is obvious that no progress can be made in such a situation until some over-all master plan is drawn that covers the mutual rights and mutual responsibilities of all. One master plan has to be substituted for four private plans. Until then, each member of the family will continue to feel hurt and damaged. No peace is possible while four separate and different blueprints exist.

Everyone who owns property demands a deed of ownership and a land survey so that he knows where his property line begins and ends. We cannot imagine a city where each has his own opinion of what he owns. Every home should be surveyed as to rights and responsibilities. When these are established, it is possible for all the members of the family to dwell together, each in the secure knowledge that his rights, privileges, and responsibilities have been fairly approved. Debatable areas of family activity must be settled so that each member is free to turn his mind to more important things.

In the situation of the two daughters, the parents had wisdom enough, at breaking point, to seek help. They were instructed to tell their daughters that they had no right to regard the family telephone as private property and that all their calls would be stopped, both incoming and outgoing, unless they themselves worked out a way to handle the telephone problem without disrupting the peace of the home or depriving their parents of the use of the phone.

The parents had to make clear to their daughters that (1) the house, and everything in it, belonged to them and not to their daughters; (2) the girls owned nothing outright, in the legal sense of ownership; (3) they were in no position to enforce their arbitrary wills as if they were laws binding on those around them; and (4) they had no right to make warfare over property that did not belong to them. As soon as the facts of true ownership were explained and the girls understood the idea of their parents' new master plan, they not only found a way to arrange their calls and their demands on the bathroom but peace descended on this home. These two sisters, who had been bitter antagonists, learned to become friendly with each other and with their parents. The entire home situation became happier for everyone.

Every child is a part of a unit at home, and his fighting is part of a mutual fight. It is asking too much to try to stop one member's aggressions until and unless the situation as a whole is put right. If a situation reaches the point where outside help is needed, the counselor should institute a family conclave of parents and children. The master plan chosen by the parents should be explained during this conclave, so that all will have the same understanding of what is expected.

Once this is done, private maps must be disregarded. All

rewards and punishments are in accordance with the observance of the master plan. Only in this way can each know his proper limits and privileges. Moreover, he always knows what he may expect of others as well as what he may not expect. This makes for security in relationships. Neither a child nor an adult can feel secure on any other basis. When this is done, no member has to keep on the alert for transgressions, for it does not take long to establish mutual respect when all know the limits.

After a reasonable, practical master plan has been in operation for a period, it will be discovered that mutual tolerance and respect will become a natural way of living. The plan will then automatically lose whatever rigidity it originally had. A fluid, healthy plan will result.

We must state again, as we did in the case of the two daughters, that the "insecurity" we see so often today in children exists because they do not know the limits of their authority and their responsibilities. They really do not know how to stop! They feel obliged to keep pushing and pushing until something stops them. They cannot relax because they know no sure boundaries to sustain them. The child who has always ended up getting his own way has no choice but to be insecure, since he has found no limits anywhere. All that "security" means is knowing *protective limits*.

The search for protective limits starts at a very young age. Let us consider a child of three who is searching for such limits. We will visit a crowded grocery store and watch what he does. This child's father and mother are in line waiting to be checked out. Their three-year-old is bent on snatching a bar of candy from the rack behind the cashier. The parents yell at him not to touch the candy, but if they happen to look in another direction for one moment, the child returns to the candy again and again. At each attempt the mother threatens punishment. But each time he repeats it, she does nothing other than to threaten him once again. His father proceeds no differently.

Here is a child who operates on his own blueprint. He cannot relax in security because his blueprint has no limits. He searches to find one. But each time a limit is promised, his parents fail him, for they do not keep their promise. By their behavior they teach him that he cannot *depend on them!* More than that, they teach him that they are liars. These parents would be horrified if they realized what their child learns from their mistaken efforts to control him. He learns that what they *do* is contrary to what they *say.* Realizing that he cannot depend on them, he is forced to keep on trying to find out if there is anything in them that is honest and dependable.

If one attempts to explain to such parents that what they need most is a master plan that marks out definite limits, they grow frightened. They have been warned so many years, now, about not "frustrating" the child that they fear this more than establishing limits for him. However, these same parents would not tear up the deed to their house, their insurance policy, their bonds, their work contracts, their tax receipts, their theater tickets. These and countless other things are only symbols of the limits by which all of us, as adults, are bound—the things that give us our feeling of security. No social life is possible without such symbols. Why should parents deny their children a secure place in the family configuration? Children need such symbols of security. Without them, children are misguided and feel more frustrated in the end.

Many parents today imagine that they will "break a child's will" if they impose limits. These parents swoon if the word "spanking" is mentioned. But it is for parents to draw up the master plan for interpersonal responsibilities so that the child will have an idea of how to express his will constructively. Then it will not need to be "broken." The child must learn to *use his will in socially useful directions.* If he insists on expressing it in ways that damage and limit others, then something must be done to show him that he may not, with impunity, hurt or burden others.

In another part of this chapter we mentioned how carefully every inch of land in a city is measured, bought, and paid for. We contrasted this with the fuzzy, indefinite boundaries of mutual rights and ownership in homes without an over-all plan or survey. We cannot emphasize too strongly the necessity for members of a family to know their proper limits in relation to one another.

Parents should insist on keeping their own rights to privacy and property so there will be no temptation for their children to try to usurp parental privileges or time. If children know how much and how little belongs to each, then they are free to settle down, inside themselves, and develop within those limits. They will not feel defrauded and angry, as they always do whenever they have tried to grab and hold on to disputed territory. It is uncertainty that makes for discontent and fighting.

If parents refuse to submit to tricks and pressures, and cling firmly to what is their own, they do not need to worry about "breaking the spirit" of a child. Children have a keen sense of fair play. They are equipped with some kind of built-in "antenna" that *senses* fair play on an action level even though it may not be expressed on a verbal level. They rarely object to disagreeable things if they are fair. This is why it is so necessary to have a master plan, so that fairness of the *total situation* is apparent to all. Each can endure privations, if necessary, if he knows they are fair.

Without a master plan, a child lives in a Netherland of Pamperdom! He commands, and his parents do his bidding, strewing sacrifices before him. Parents would not do this if they were aware that such sacrifices are basically asocial because they mean that someone does less than his fair share. The person for whom sacrifices are made usually becomes more selfish as a result. We appreciate only what we have helped to create. The selfish child is headed for trouble and unhappiness. He enslaves himself, his parents, and others.

8

COLONIAL STATUS IS NOT GOOD
FOR PARENTS

Parents who have sacrificed themselves to pamper their children have succeeded only in rearing children with "larceny
in their hearts." They have invited colonial status for themselves. They have put themselves in much the same position
as were our early colonists in America, before the Revolu-
tion.

The colonists were subjects of Great Britain. (Pampering
parents are subjects of their children.) In pre-Revolutionary
days, taxes and demands kept increasing. The colonists were
forced to provide advantages for their British rulers, with
little return for extortion. (Pampered children grow to be
clever extortionists.) There came a day when the colonists
decided they would tolerate no more taxation without repre-
sentation. They strengthened their resolve and issued a Declaration of Independence that stated, in essence, that they
were willing to be friends, but no longer degraded servants.
They fought a short war of independence. Thereafter the
colonists' rights to equality were fixed and there could be a
friendly exchange.

Such an "out" is possible for parents with "larcenous"
children in their family—children who expect to get their
own way in everything and who nag and whine when, for one

reason or another, they don't. Exploited parents need only to issue a Declaration of Independence and fight a short war to gain the status of equality with their children. A long war is not necessary. Enslaved parents have only to refuse to pay tribute any longer. Then they must concentrate on "passive resistance against exploitation," instead of trying to persuade their children to "do the right things." Whoever heard of anyone consulting his jailer about how to escape and win his freedom!

A "Bill of Rights" makes for healthy parents and healthy children. Here is a sample one for any parents who want freedom from colonial status. Adopt it and watch what happens!

(1) YOUR RIGHTS ARE AS IMPORTANT AS YOUR CHILD'S, IF NOT MORE SO!

Because you are an adult, your responsibility is far greater than that of a child. You are responsible to the child and to the outside world. You must have authority commensurate with the responsibility you have to carry. The child should not have more authority in those things that *pertain to you* than you have— if as much. The Bible says, "Do not muzzle the ox that treads out the grain"—if you need the sanction of Holy Writ to take your rights!

(2) TAKE YOUR FULL SHARE EVERY TIME!

There is no better way to teach children to know you have rights than to use your rights. They *see* you use them. Rights that are not used are like a vacant lot that is not protected; children move into it and dump refuse on it. The child will respect your value when he sees you assert your worth, and he thereby learns to respect the value and worth of those with whom he comes in contact.

(3) HAVE A PRIVATE LIFE OF YOUR OWN AND HAVE SOME FUN EVERY DAY!

Recreation means re-creation or the renewal of the spirit. You cannot be a good fellow man to anyone, least of all to your children, if your morale is broken. Life loses all meaning when joy goes out of it, and when that happens, we become blind as moles.

(4) KEEP YOUR PERSONAL AMBITION SEPARATE FROM YOUR CHILDREN'S AMBITIONS!

Do not try to fulfill your life's ambition through your children. Find fulfillment in terms of your own accomplishments, not theirs. Then you will not need to hate your children for "defrauding" you. And they will not need to hate you for smothering their inner gleam!

(5) LEARN TO MIND YOUR OWN BUSINESS AND MAKE IT UNPROFITABLE FOR YOUR CHILDREN NOT TO DO LIKEWISE!

Remember that children are not your possessions. They are only transients or visitors who pass through your home on their way to the outside world, where they will be expected to be a help and not a burden. As husband and wife, you have your whole lives to spend together after your children have ended their visit in your home. Your relationship, one to the other, should be as important as your relationship to your children. Nothing should diminish your interest in each other. Your children should never be allowed to steal the interest of one of you from the other. Do not your children's keepers be, and do not allow yourself to be kept by them!

Whenever parents, entrapped and enslaved by their children, have dared to adopt a Bill of Rights, they have found themselves on safe and sound ground—free, at last. For when a condition of mutual profit for all is made the way of life in a home, parents do not exploit children nor do children exploit parents. Democracy reigns!

Not all parents dare accept such a proposal, even though they have been defeated and degraded by their domineering children. They are resistant even when given assurance that many of their family problems will be dissipated or will evaporate into thin air. After years of training in catering to, and in servitude to, their children, they find it most difficult to consider being "just friends" with their children and living on a fifty-fifty basis with them.

This is especially true of mothers who have devoted themselves to their children in an effort to live vicariously through them. They have minded their children's business to such an extent that they have no orientation outside their homes. When their children, whom they have made dependent, begin to fail in school or otherwise embarrass them in front of neighbors, relatives, and friends, they often feel the need to seek guidance help. But they become resistant and frightened when it is suggested that now they must "untie their apron strings" and allow their children to stand on their own two feet. If they were to allow their children to be independent of them, they would become members of that Great Army of the Emotionally Unemployed. They have had their noses in their children's business so long that they have not developed a single interest of their own. Although they have come to resent their leaning children, they discontinue treatment in order to avoid taking such a drastic new step as establishing a Bill of Rights. Sometimes they go elsewhere, looking for more elaborate "labels" and "deeper meaning" to their problems—as if, in labeling or describing a problem, there were some magic that would make it disappear. Their own lack of courage in the face of the "unknown" is, of course, transmitted to their children.

Mrs. Z. was in the Army of the Emotionally Unemployed. Her husband made a good deal of money, but this kept him so busy he had little time to devote to his wife or his daughter, Sue. His wife hired the best of help. Since she had nothing to do but spend his money, she became a perfectionist in all matters concerning her home and her family.

She made no friends, nor did she engage in any activities or hobbies of a self-expressive nature. This does not mean that Mrs. Z. had no ambition. She had an overweening ambition to make a good impression, but—as is typical in all such cases—she had a corresponding fear of making mistakes. Therefore Mrs. Z. did nothing on her own, for fear of being found less than perfect.

Because time hung heavy on Mrs. Z.'s hands, she began to live vicariously through her eight-year-old daughter, Sue. She imposed her perfectionist standards and her own fears on this child. She nagged her constantly to "do better." Under her mother's barrage of admonitions, Sue became unsure of herself and commenced to close up like a clam. Finally Sue said and did as little as possible in order not to provoke uncomplimentary remarks from her mother.

Mrs. Z. felt frustrated in the face of Sue's passivity and took her to a psychiatrist in the hope that he would wave a magic wand of some kind and make Sue a perfect child. The psychiatrist explained that she must relax her endless criticism of the child. He attempted to divert Mrs. Z. to some independent activity of her own, so that her restless ambition could be turned toward her own fulfillment rather than toward her daughter. When Mrs. Z. did not move in the direction of his advice, he urged her to undergo therapy herself, so that she could get rid of her own lack of courage for self-expression. Mrs. Z. refused.

The psychiatrist continued in his efforts to help the child, but Sue showed slight progress. Why should she venture forth when she knew that no matter what she did her mother would heap criticism upon her? Under such circumstances, why shouldn't Sue prefer to remain in her bombproof shelter? At the end of six months Mrs. Z. grew impatient and critical of the psychiatrist because there was no dramatic change in Sue. She discontinued treatment—but not her destructive meddling with her daughter.

Mrs. Z. does not walk alone. There are many parents who feel humiliated by the lack of success of their dependent children. But they find it is often easier to run away from the problem than to face up to any of their own responsibilities. Playing an "ostrich" role is more comfortable. In other words, many parents find it preferable to nag and push their children, with the hope that the children will cover up their own inadequacies and failures as far as the outside world is concerned. This is too much to expect of children. We cannot expect them to change and to improve in courage—that is, move in new directions in the face of possible "danger"—if their parents dare not do as much themselves.

There is no remedy that will cut off the dependence of children until parents gain their own independence. Many parents might dare tackle cutting off the child's dependency if they could only do it a bit at a time. This would be no kindness, however, for it would only stimulate a child to fight harder and longer at each cutting-off point. If it becomes necessary to cut off the tail of a puppy, it is not kinder to cut it off a half inch at a time! The severing of a dependency relationship is always painful—otherwise it would have solved itself.

Let us consider how easy it really is to initiate this process. One of the best ways to illustrate the point is to consider a child known as a "feeding problem." The child's purpose in refusing to eat is that in this way he can dominate his parents and force them to make him the center of attention. Thus each meal becomes a battle which the child wins only because his parents feel they dare not let him go without food. They are certain that the child would never eat if he were not wheedled or coaxed to do so. This, of course, is sheer nonsense. No normal child will voluntarily starve himself to death. The child will not learn to eat independently as long as his parents are willing to be manipulated by his refusal to eat.

When parents gain enough courage to turn the responsibility for eating over to the child, the problem solves itself. If they do not invite their child to the table at all and if no one notices his absence—as if it were intended to let him starve—this shocking change of attitude is such surprise to the child that at first he is bewildered. However, when he finds he cannot gain any illicit domination over his parents by the misuse of mealtimes, nor can he upset them, he soon finds the remnants of his natural appetite, urging him to eat. When he is convinced that no one can be intimidated by his lack of appetite, he begins to eat with relish. After all, he gets hungry and he needs to eat. Courage is as infectious as cowardice.

Parents will remain defeated until they reverse their direction and move toward, instead of away from, the area in which they have been defeated. Parents have to barricade the avenues of escape for those children who have been allowed to run away from the proper use of their functions. They must agree mutually on the handling of the child and stick to their agreement, because children are quick to find the loopholes where parents disagree and play one parent against the other. Parents must present a united front on those matters that pertain to their children, regardless of the extent to which they may have conflicts on other matters.

Parents succeed when they become entirely matter-of-fact about their children. When parents lack courage they sponsor lack of courage in their children. They train them for future misery and make emotional cripples of them!

9

EMOTIONALLY CRIPPLED CHILDREN
LEAN ON PARENTAL "CRUTCHES"

A child who makes a problem out of eating or any other natural function is a child who is emotionally dependent and is using his parents as a crutch. Most parents have been defeated in helping the whole child because they have tried to cure the symptom currently presented. There is no way for a parent to "cure" bed-wetting, night terrors, or sleepwalking, for example, by concentrating on these symptoms, per se. One often hears a parent say such things as: "He is a good child, except that he fails in school." Or we hear, "He is fine at school and at home but he still sucks his thumb at the age of ten." This is like saying, "She's a little bit pregnant!" Parents who speak in this fashion do not see the many other ways in which a child expresses his dependency during the whole day and night.

When is a symptom not a symptom of emotional crippling? Some children are born spastic. Some lose limbs early in life. Many are crippled by polio. There are numberless things that can happen to a child that will damage some of his functions physically. Some illnesses leave impairments of heart, eyes, ears, or some other organ. How shall we differentiate a legitimate physical symptom from a similar symptom that indicates emotional disaster on the horizon? A child may begin vomiting as the first sign of a real illness. Or he may vomit over the days or years with no physical findings evident at any time. And sometimes symptoms make their first appearance with an illness but persist long after the child has been cured.

It is not always easy to tell, in the beginning, whether a symptom is physical or emotional, and it is always wise to check any abnormal symptom with your child's doctor. However, physical ills tend to run their course and disappear, and when they are gone their symptoms are gone, too. We must always suspect any symptom that persists over a period of time when there is no other evidence of illness. In such cases, it almost always means that emotional crippling is getting under way.

The body seems to have a will to be strong and healthy. We have only to cite such individuals as Helen Keller, who became deaf and blind in early childhood, to see that even the worst physical handicaps cannot deter a child if he is guarded from emotional involvements with his symptoms. In contrast to Helen Keller, there are many people who were born physically intact, except for a disfiguring nose or something of like nature, and yet have *used* these bagatelles as excuses for emotional crippling throughout life.

The big factor in differentiation, then, lies in the question of the child's *using the symptoms* to get special help, preferment, and undue consideration in relation to those around him. Many children are chronically phlegmatic and listless at home and at school but can run like a deer to catch a fly ball in a baseball game. Many vomit daily in winter as a protest against school, but are miraculously well in summer. The symptoms must be fitted into the whole picture in order to understand when they are genuinely physical and when they constitute an evasion.

Parents have to view with new eyes the whole day and night as a continuum. If they do this, they find that their so-called

single-problem children are depending on them all day long
and also feel entitled to use them as crutches at night. They
will find that the child who seems to have only one problem
has many. Perhaps he fails to pick up after himself, cannot
decide what to wear, forgets his hat and overshoes, dawdles in
dressing, cries easily when disappointed, will not allow his
door to be shut, is generally clumsy, as well as dozens of other
things. Each of these little things is a trick device to compel
the parent to be a crutch. Each is a way of domination. The
bedwetting, nightmare, or sleepwalking is only the nighttime continuation of the same daytime aggression.

The child tries a bit of everything at one time or another. If
he finds his parents ticklish at any point, he simply makes a
note of this and employs those things that made the most impression. One is not apt, for instance, to find noneaters in
very poor families where food is scarce. In such a situation
it would be of no advantage for a child not to eat. His brothers and sisters would be only too happy if he ate less! Food
problems arise only with parents who are overimpressed with
their small knowledge of nutrition. The human race is millions of years old and has survived thousands of devastating
famines. We refuse to die as long as we have even a crumb to
eat. It is only comparatively recently that man has eaten with
any degree of regularity. Some primitive tribes even today eat
well only on those fortunate occasions when a hunter brings
down some game. At other times they go relatively hungry
except for chance bugs or grubs, berries or roots. It is ridiculous for parents to be terrified if a child skips a meal or two.
The child will gladly undereat if it is the one way in which he
can pinpoint the parents' Achilles heel—and get a response!

Many counselors become fascinated with the kind of symptom a child presents and try to find specific causes for the
symptom. They try to find out whether the child was frightened by a lion when he visited the zoo years before, or

whether he may have heard his parents making love in bed at night. There is no limit to which some counselors will not go in conjuring up probable causes for the various symptoms children employ in their fight for domination of their parents.

It is not the lion at the zoo that causes the nightmare, and it isn't the creaking of the springs in the next bed. If the child is *using* any symptom—this one or that one—we may be sure he is doing so because he has tested it and found it strikes fear in the heart of the parent. In some civilizations, for example, sexual activities of children are considered of no significance at all; they are allowed to do whatever they please in this respect. In such cultures, parents of adolescent daughters do not chill with fear if their child is not in sight at all times. But in our civilization, for instance, the fear of sexual exploits is one of the strongest taboos we know, and therefore it is an ideal weapon for a child. However, most of the so-called sexual delinquents are children who have always managed to dominate their parents in one way or another and have found in sex the strongest of all weapons to use in their fight for dominance. If parents have always given in to all the demands of their children, it is useless to try to draw the line in a *single* area. The child who has had his way all the time, in every way, will not stand being denied sexual activity. The "poor eater," the bed-wetter, the thumb-sucker, the school failure, the sex delinquent—these and other problem children are manifesting emotional crippling. The psyches of these children are supercharged with emotional dependency and are broadcasting static (their hostilities)! These are the children who have been allowed to use parents as crutches in many areas of life and have had no training in self-reliance or independence. If a parent has not already begun to train a child for self-sufficiency, there is no better time to begin than *today!* In the beginning, only one maxim needs to

be kept in mind: No parent should do for a child anything
that the child is physically old enough and able to do for
himself. Even with children who are ill or with those who
have cerebral palsy and similar organic handicaps, we must
do less each day so that they will be obliged to learn how to
help themselves more each day. They need to feel somewhat
deprived so that they have the incentive to grow up. There is
a truism that applies in this instance: "Ambition is like hunger—it obeys no law but its own appetite."

Any display of anxiety on a child's part is apt to make today's parent have heart failure. This is one of the neatest
tricks a child may employ. A couple of nightmares and sweats
is almost a guarantee for a child who intends to keep a parent
from winning independence and who intends to keep himself
infantile. In such outbreaks, of course, there may be a physio-
logical process at work, but one should also consider that
there may be a psychological factor involved. Anything as
dramatic as nightmares and night sweats that is purely physical would probably be accompanied by a temperature and
would develop shortly into a recognized illness. But such oc-
currences, when psychologically based, find the child essentially well the following day—especially if there is something
he wants to do that day.

If we investigate the *purpose* of anxiety, we can see that it
is a very effective weapon of parental control for any child
who has grown used to being helped and pampered. Unbridled anger is the same sort of device. We may assume that in
any physical symptom there is the possibility of genuine physical disorder, but we should not overlook the fact that the
child may be making an effort to achieve a very definite goal.
If we cater to each and every anxiety and temper outburst of
a child, we lead him to consider that every person is an instrument for his convenience. As he grows older he will not
find people outside his home who are willing to serve him in

any such fashion. They will resent his attempts to cast them in such roles and will reject him justly. He, in turn, will call the world unjust because it does not heed him. For this reason, and for their own future peace, parents should be wary of a child's attempts to enslave them in this manner.

On this score, we should consider the one time of day during which parents lose more ground than at almost any other: the interval between supper and bedtime. This probably occurs because parents have been overimpressed with the notion that it's during the twilight hour that a child needs special attention. What nonsense! After the final meal of the day, parents should be free of their children so that they have time together as man and wife to renew their own mutual interests. The mother has been tied down all day serving the needs of her family. The father has been caught all day in the problems of making a living in a busy world. Both need a few hours together, free of cares, so they may relax their efforts. They need time to be interested in the welfare of the community as a whole. They should not have to face a period of even greater stress on top of all they have endured during the day. Otherwise they go from day to day like galley slaves, chained always to the same oar.

Parents should so train their children that they seek their own part of the home and engage in their own activities immediately after dinner. Nor should children be allowed, once in their own quarters, to behave in a way that demands the attention of parents or distracts them at this time. When schoolwork or other chores have been completed, they should be allowed to play relatively quietly at whatever they choose, without parental snooping, as long as it does not disrupt the peace and quiet of those around them.

This is the way it should be. No child should be allowed to become overstimulated after the dinner hour. Parents should insist on having the hours after dinner as their own, and free of interruptions, so that a gentle boredom may descend on a child. Natural fatigue will have a chance to assert itself. Soon a child's eyelids will grow heavy and he will go off to bed before sleep overtakes him. No policeman has to attend to his retirement!

However, what usually happens in the child-centered home is quite different. Everyone becomes overstimulated. Let us consider what happens in a family where there are two children. Warfare between the washed and the unwashed starts at the dinner table. Complaints about the food are made. In the old days, when we complained about the toughness of the meat, our father said, "It's tougher where there's none!" That ended the complaints. But today mother trots out to the kitchen and slaves over the hot stove again and again to satisfy the complaints of both children. Then come yells about the behavior of brother or sister, and this phase ends up in kicks under the table and often in fisticuffs. Irritability mounts by the clock. No wonder so many fathers have labeled their dinner tables as wonderful "ulcer factories!"

When dinner is finished, the living room becomes the battleground. Each child fights for the "best" chair or place on the divan before the television set. Then there ensues a clamor for a preferred program, and no one agrees with anyone else about which it is to be. Parents shout, shame, cajole, nag, and end up by giving in to whichever child makes the most noise. It's purely accidental if parents are able to see the program they want on the television set they sweated to purchase. As the evening passes, parents and children become more stimulated and aggressive. Nerves are frayed and acquire a razor's edge.

Next comes the battle as to who goes to bed first. The younger feels damaged because he is expected to retire a half hour before the older child. He becomes the center of a struggle to get him in and out of the bathroom and into bed. It is a paltry younger child, indeed, who cannot win this battle by dawdling, screaming for water or milk, yelling that there are lions under his bed, and similar alarms and excursions. A favorite trick is to keep running into the living room demanding endlessly, "Daddy, kiss me again!" Such kissing expeditions should be labeled properly; they should be called "the kiss of death!"

By this time the older child has grown equally resentful because the younger child has gained the half hour of extra attention, at the expense of his dignity as an "elder statesman." So he must stay up that much longer in order to preserve his status. Meanwhile, the younger one is having a bad time keeping himself awake in order to defeat the older one's attempts to be superior.

When at last the warfare has ceased, the parents are exhausted. The bedlam has lifted the level of adrenalin in their own blood streams so that they are now ready to cut each other's jugular veins! In any case, they wish sullenly that they had had sense enough to remain single in the first place and had left this "love and security" business to someone else! Like the beaten slaves they are, they finally crawl off to bed, only to face another day and another night of torture at the hands of their self-centered children in their child-centered home.

This whole situation somehow is justified by mothers on the grounds that children need this contact with their fathers. There is supposed to be some magic that comes simply from sitting in the same room together. But it is difficult to figure out what good it does children to discover that they can torture, dominate, and frustrate their fathers as well as their mothers. By the time these children are finally driven to bed, at their own convenience, they are filled with anger at their mother, their father, and each other. This is hardly the basis for a satisfactory relationship with anyone. Certainly the human relationships in such homes are not good and are not "humanly straight."

Deep and enduring human relationships are not made by the clock by *x* hours a day with father. Fighting children do not profit from exposure to a father if they spend their time emasculating him of whatever manhood he may have. It is only a travesty to assume that parents are the heads of the family and are authority figures if, in reality, children have the upper hand in every single encounter.

The contacts in family life should be as functional and reasonable as the relationships of all good citizens in the outside world should be, or the contacts between any busy and productive people. A family normally meets at mealtimes, week ends, and on holidays. This is more time than we usually spend with people outside our families. If relationships in the family are not strained by conflict, we may be sure that the members of the family will find plenty of mutual enrichment at such times, because no disruptions destroy the interchange of feelings and ideas. If members of a family are emotionally healthy, they will enjoy one another to the fullest and then promptly scatter to their own individual pursuits when meals or holidays are over. There will be no neurotic clinging to one another for mere propinquity. True companionships *continue to exist* even while individuals are separated and doing their own private jobs. Companionship means mutual appreciation of like-minded and like-feeling individuals, regardless of whether they are physically present or far apart. Sitting in the same room does not of necessity result in companionship. As a matter of fact, propinquity alone is more apt to produce boredom—as it does in far too many families today.

It is not necessary to insert endless case histories at this point to illustrate how children "shop around" for tricks and techniques to enslave and dominate their parents. However, to clarify this particular problem, it might be well to tell the story of Tommy's temper tantrum. It gives us a succinct picture of how a child tests the whole surrounding terrain to find soft spots he can use for goofing. Tommy was four and the only child of wise parents. His mother was not the kind of gal to feed anyone's neurosis, not even Tommy's—if he thought of starting one. One afternoon she was visiting on the lawn with a neighbor who had a son Tommy's age. The children were playing together while the parents visited with each other. Suddenly the neighbor's boy threw a temper tantrum. Tommy watched in amazement as the child kicked and beat his fists and as the mother petted and placated him. Tommy's mother noticed his entranced interest and suspected he was putting this display away in his file cabinet of not-to-be-forgotten items. She was correct in this observation and was prepared, therefore, for what followed.

That night Tommy and his parents were eating dinner. Tommy got down from his chair to go across the living room to the bathroom. In the middle of the living room—in full sight, of course—he threw himself down on his belly and started screaming, just as his little friend had done. His father was taken by surprise and was halfway out of his chair when he caught a high-sign from his wife that he should not bite on this one! He sat back, and husband and wife continued their conversation as if nothing were happening there on the living-room rug. Poor Tommy was stranded out on a limb with his blooming temper tantrum!

Anyone who can recall the last temper tantrum he had, remembers that it was hard work! And additionally, it is certainly unprofitable for any actor to play to an empty house. Poor Tommy was spending energy without appreciation. It did not take him long to realize that the jig was up. In a few moments he reared up on his elbow as a prelude to standing up again. His mother heard him remark to himself as he did so, "Well, this isn't getting me anywhere!" With that, he went off to the bathroom as he had intended to do before the temptation to entrap his parents occurred to him. And so this little Columbus failed to land on his parents' territory and had to sail back to his own resources!

Nothing that has been written in this chapter should be taken to mean that parents should try to control everything a child says and does. Such obedience-training programs may be necessary for dogs but certainly not for children. However, since parents have the responsibility for their children, they should keep enough authority to fulfill their jobs as parents. They should set-up *minimum* demands that are *binding on all the children alike*. The yardstick for parents to keep in mind in establishing minimum demands should be based on training children to be more self-sufficient and helpful rather than permitting them to make unnecessary trouble for others. Unless this is done, a home is not a home; it is just a battleground.

10

BOOBY TRAPS FOR PARENTS!

A home that is a battleground is planted with booby traps likely to explode at any time in the faces of parents. Parents whose homes have become or are on the way to becoming battlegrounds need some kind of radar equipment to detect them and mine sweepers to get rid of them. This chapter is devoted to describing some of the dangerous booby traps for parents to avoid, in addition to the twilight-hour booby trap. It might be called a chapter devoted to training parents how to mind their own business and to train their children to do likewise.

OVERPROTECTION

In general, children would grow up with little difficulty if we were not forever interfering with them. Every child needs a constant supply of "intelligent neglect" so that he has a chance, and can develop a need, to discover his world at first hand, without being misled by adult interference. To be sure, adults must do for children those things that cannot be expected of them at their particular age. But it is the parents' job always to give a little less help each day in every way, so the child will always find it necessary to struggle to help himself at all times. It is this struggle that makes him strong and prepares him for the world he must face.

Overprotection is a deterrent to the proper preparation of a child for the outside world, and yet it is adults' most frequent way of not minding their own business. Ambitious parents hope to speed up the natural process of development of their children by removing all possible risks and all possible dangers from their paths. Nowadays, the least sniffle is regarded by overprotective parents as potential death! Any trifling deviation in the child's interests or activities is a major defeat for the parent, who feels he must eradicate it at once. If the child eats an ounce less than the parents feel necessary, pressure is brought to bear at once to force him to eat more. In short, the child becomes the center of constant and anxious attention. In reality, he is being thwarted at every turn by the limiting chains of dependency and interference that the parents put upon him. By the time he should be free of such chains, they have grown so strong that he can use them to tie the parents to him. Since he has never learned to think or act for himself, he begins to "need" his parents to think and act for him.

In essence, the child has little chance to do otherwise. Since his parents have deprived him of the chance to make his own mistakes, he has not learned how to overcome difficulties by himself. He later finds himself unable to cope with children his own age who are not so chained. He becomes jealous of their successes. Since he feels unable to expand in the direction in which they are going, he uses his dependency whims or chains to pull the parents closer to him. They must remain his companions and servants because he has no confidence in his own ability to meet reality without their omnipotent assistance. They are his crutches. In time he becomes completely adult-centered and learns only to mind other people's business, whereas he should be child-centered and should have learned to mind his own business.

EARLY ILLNESS

The aftermath of a protracted early illness in the life of any child represents a dangerous trap for parents. Of necessity, parents must make his situation as easy as possible so he will recover. While he is ill he misses the normal opportunities he would have to develop independence. And at the same time he discovers how "precious" he is in the eyes of his family. When he gets well he may discover that his age-mates have surpassed him in the rough games of childhood. He "feels strange" now that the time has come for him to join their common life again. More often than not, he will try to regain the protected position he enjoyed while truly ill. If his parents are overprotective, they make it easy for him to *simulate* illness, and he finds he can always retire to his bed as soon as he is faced with small difficulties in school or at play. This gives him a temporary advantage in the family over his brothers and sisters. They become resentful and jealous. They complain. In the end, everybody is minding everybody else's business and nobody is accomplishing anything.

DETHRONEMENT

We can well imagine what a threat it is to a first-born, dependent child to have to share the use of his private crutch when another baby is born. He becomes as a "prince dethroned by an enemy who usurps his kingdom." For the newborn infant demands total care when it is awake and scarcely less attention when it is asleep. In short, the private crutch becomes almost the sole property of the infant, whereas the need of the older child for the crutch is in no way lessened. He responds at once to the threat with some effort to win the parents away from the infant.

How can an already dependent older child, in need of his crutch, win against an infant? He has to increase his dependency, of course. He discovers that in short order. He discovers that the trick is to beat the baby at its own game. He begins to train himself to become a bigger baby or, in other words, to out-baby the baby. He may find it's a good idea to wet himself by day and by night. He may lose the ability, if he had it, to dress himself. He commences to dawdle endlessly to force his parents to be occupied with him. He creates night terrors and wakes up screaming. Sometimes he openly attacks the infant, so that he must be watched constantly. He starts a campaign of crying for nothing at all. He develops anxieties about all kinds of imaginary dangers that he never thought of before. He tries every kind of simulated helplessness. If any single one of these ruses succeeds in getting the precious attention he seeks, he knows he has struck pay dirt and he clings to it like a miner to his stake. It then becomes a means by which he can worry his parents and divert attention from the baby to himself. His persistent infantilism usually leads to punishment, but he will welcome even punishment if that is the only way he can get his beloved attention.

The dethroned, dependent oldest may even commit petty crimes. Some such children steal, lie, cheat, develop attention-getting sex practices, or do any number of other things to oblige others to be occupied with them. Almost anything will do if it will bring back the Lost Kingdom.

And, of course, one of the most effective ways of forcing parents to be concerned is to do poorly in school. Any dependent child soon discovers that the teacher quickly reports his inadequacies to the parents. The parents' pride is such that they feel humiliated and begin to help with his school-work (in many cases doing it for him). Once they start that, they dare not stop lest the child become a worse school failure than he already is. By this time a vicious circle closes around the child and the parents. At last the crutch is secured firmly in the hands of the child. If and when the parents try to free themselves from this additional slavery, the child has only to produce another school failure to reduce his parents to their original position of servitude.

So it is that the dependent child finds that a consistent "I can't" gives him command over his parents as well as his teacher. He does not consider trying to compensate his weakness, for he is determined not to give up his commanding position over his elders. Though he may be most unhappy that he is not able to be a part of his own age group, he feels it is too late, now, to start trying to stand on his own feet after so many years of leaning on a crutch.

RIVALRY

Meanwhile the younger child has noted the peculiar power of the older child over the parents. This stimulates him to a variety of ways in which he may bring counterpressure on the parents and keep the kingdom from falling back into the hands of its original heir. Any number of things can stimulate rivalry, once the battlelines have been drawn.

One of the most frequent traps for parents is constant talebearing and quarreling, kicks under the table, complaints that one has been favored with a larger piece of meat, yelps that privileges have been granted one or the other, and a host of similar things. This constant nettling of each other is intended to, and does, trap the parents. Misguided parents like to settle these claims individually. They run from one to the other in a vain effort to restore quiet in the home. The harder the parents try to be fair, the worse the fighting becomes. One child imagines that the other is being preferred, and accusations fly. When the parents attempt to even up the situation, the child who fears himself unfavored brings in a bigger claim against his parents. All this leads only to the children's becoming more watchful of the parents and each other. Finally each word and each situation has to be weighed on a jeweler's scale!

A certain rivalry exists in every family where there are two or more children. It is inevitable. Jealousy between children of the same parents has been with us ever since Cain and Abel. Each child in the family wants to be the only and the favored child. He resents the efforts of the other child or children to win attention from the parents. Whether this is a mild condition or a severe curse to a family depends entirely on how the parents recognize and handle the situation as it arises.

Too many parents today fail to recognize the devastating effects of so-called sibling rivalry in their homes. They have become so accustomed to it and its social complications that they often accept it as the normal state of affairs. When asked about it, they reply that there is the "usual" bickering that one would expect among the children. However, on investigation, one is very apt to find that there is continuous fussin'-and-feudin' and that this is impoverishing the personality and the productivity of each child.

In these homes, for example, the children watch from ambush to make sure the others do not get away with anything, while each tries to get away with everything for himself. If the mother asks Bobby to empty the garbage or to run an errand, he cries, "Make Jack do it. I emptied it last time." Then an argument starts about who did what when, and in the end Mother empties the garbage herself! She is the one who is damaged, but the children get their dishes of ice cream for supper just as if they had not disrupted family life over trivia. Thus they are encouraged to do as little as possible, as a matter of prestige, instead of each increasing his activity and usefulness.

About the only just way to handle such rivalries is to penalize equally all parties to the crime. It never settles anything to attempt to find out who started what or which one is guilty, for in that direction lie the complaints of preference and favoritism. The only solution is to have an unwritten law that the peace and quiet of the home may not be disturbed because the children are needling one another. Let it be understood that they have permission to fight outdoors and may the best man win—but they are not allowed to come running in to yap about winnings or losings. If children are held equally guilty when they have disturbed the peace of the home with fighting, they learn not to start anything they can't finish. When children discover that their parents will not support one against the other and will, in addition, make trouble for both of them if they fight inside the home, then they learn to live together.

All parents who question such a procedure are encouraged to try it! If parents are serious about the matter, they soon discover that these fights are bait to hook them. When children have permission to fight outdoors, the fighting soon ceases. Who likes to put on a command performance with no audience? Countless parents know that when they are away from the house (if their children ever allow them to go out), the children get along quite well. They begin to fight only when their parents return. This is proof that such fighting serves only to embroil the parents. If parents are honest about this, they soon realize all too clearly that they are the *prize* to be won! If there is no such prize, rivalry and competitive fighting fall to an irreducible minimum.

Many parents who feel such rivalry is unavoidable at home

and is a part of the child's essential nature fail to see another important point. That is that these same children who do not know how to act at home find no difficulty being quiet at a church service. If they are invited to a stranger's home, without their parents, their host often phones the parents, following the visit, to report on their beautiful manners and considerate behavior. However, once home, they turn into the same unmitigated little monsters!

Now, there is no disease that can be put on and off at will. The only thing at work in such situations is that parents have not penalized destructive behavior in the home. If parents do not demand from their children the same amount of consideration the children give to strangers, why should they be so surprised that they receive less? It is indeed amazing how much less mutual respect and consideration exist among members of a family and relatives than among strangers. If strangers were subjected to such exploitation, they would neither feel obliged to submit nor would they accept such abusive treatment. Nor should parents. When their freedom is restricted and their pursuit of happiness is destroyed by the private feuds of their children, it is time for them to act.

It was once believed that if parents would explain to a child that he was to have a little brother or sister, he would not resent it. He was to be told that his parents had enjoyed him so much that they wanted to increase their happiness. This was supposed to avoid jealous competition and rivalry. It did not work. Why should it? Needless to say, if a man tells his wife he has loved her so much that he now plans to bring another wife into the home to "increase his happiness," she would not be immune to jealousy. On the contrary, the fight would just begin—in exactly the same fashion as it does with children.

Children of the same family should not interfere with each other's business. They should be encouraged to play with, and engage in activities with, age-mates outside the home. It is not good, for example, to have a boy of eight playing exclusively with his four-year-old sister. When this happens, either sister must strain to keep up with her brother, or he patterns his behavior on her babyish ways.

Nor should parents feel the need to descend to the level of their children. If parents devote themselves to the child's world, they lose touch with reality. This does not mean, of course, that parents should never take their children anywhere or show any interest in them. It means that any interest they have should be voluntary and not the result of coercion. The entire family can enjoy activities as a family only if each member is allowed to enjoy his activities as an individual. Each member of the family should have his own interests, appropriate to his age and development. A happy family is one in which each has something to do and does it. An unhappy family is one in which everyone minds everyone else's business, and bickerings and jealousies run rampant.

JEALOUSY

There is no end to the things that can stimulate jealousy between siblings. Parents or grandparents may have a real preference for one child in the family. The other is certain to resent this and will surely make trouble of one kind or another. Often one child is more attractive than the others, and strangers will praise it without noting its brothers or sisters. Or one may be precocious and win much admiration. As long as children have a dependent attitude toward their parents, any special notice given one above the other will feed the flames of jealousy. Jealousy so inflamed leads to sabotage or open fighting.

One of the most common ways parents have of sponsoring jealousy amongst their children is for them to forbid the older child to protect himself against the competition of the younger. This ties the older child's hands and gives the younger complete license to get in his hair. The younger demands all the privileges and possessions of the older one. If the older one forgets and strikes the younger child or takes something away from him, there is a battle. At this point the parents enter in and again forbid such retaliation on the part of the older. This leads him to feel that a great injustice has been done him, and it _proves_ (just as he has suspected all along) that the parents have a greater love for the younger child. This starts a slow burn of impotent anger in the older child, which eventually flares in all directions and sears his spirit. By the same token, the younger is thus encouraged to become more aggressive, since he knows he is immune to punishment.

Among so-called lower animals, the younger ones learn from the beginning to keep at a safe distance from older animals until they have become equally strong. Nature's way is still a good one for humans to follow. The younger should not believe he has exactly the same rights, privileges, and immunities as the older, just as no child should be led to believe his rights, privileges, and immunities are the same as his parents'. The younger child must learn to wait. To grow into the position of equal. Parents should not present equality to him on a platter, by limiting the older's rights to the level of the younger's. When younger children are not completely protected against older ones, it does not take them long to learn that they should not aspire to things they cannot manage independently. This keeps them from "getting too big for their britches" and also stimulates them to want to grow up. And at the same time, the older is not discouraged by being unjustly held back to the more infantile level of the younger. The best wisdom the younger can have is to keep out of the way of the older.

Too many parents fail to mind their own business in this respect. They feel that their children should grow up loving one another. They interfere with the natural process by which older and younger animals are kept apart by nature. Animals of different ages have different problems and different interests. No good can come from trying to mix these different levels. Each child should have his own toys, friends, interests, and activities. It does not promote good will and understanding among children to hold all the members of the family to the same level. On the contrary, it raises endless problems that cannot be solved. In families where children are made independent of each other, they can truly afford to like each other and to respect the rights of others. They do not need to become jealous of the success of others, for they are creating successes of their own from which to draw satisfaction.

This philosophy of "brotherly love"—or lack thereof—will give rise to cries of anguish from parents who are determined that all their children shall love one another, even if they have to punish them to make them do so! Unfortunately, such parental ambition is beyond the power of humans to accomplish. God himself has not won the love of everyone. In many churches there are still empty pews. Just as it is possible to say that men of all races should love one another because we share the same earth together, it is possible to say that brothers and sisters should love one another. It is certainly safer if they do. But it is not possible to force or to legislate love on anyone, or demand that he give it to another. The best we can do is to set up conditions that promote such growth. Self-sufficient children, like self-sufficient nations, have less reason to start a fracas and are more likely to like one another and to enjoy good relations. It is rivalry that starts and continues trouble between children—just as it is between nations.

Love is like a wild bird. If we want it to nest in a birdhouse of our creation in our yard, we must make the conditions right. Cats and other prowlers must be discouraged. Then there is some chance that the bird may investigate the nesting place we have built for its home and approve of it. Jealous rivalry is a kind of "noise" that frightens love away. Parents who want their children to enjoy one another can accomplish this result only by making each child independent of the other—that is, nonleaning and nondemanding. Love itself is the by-produce of good human relationships. It can never be a thing apart. It cannot be achieved in any family by "smacking" Junior for slapping little sister when she has wrecked the block house he built, and then admonishing him that he must "love his darling little sister." If grownups force him to kiss and make up, it only increases his hatred—as would be the case with any adult.

The same laws of friendship govern children in a family as govern adults in the selection of their friends. All adults know many wonderful, worthy people of different ages and walks of life. But this does not necessarily mean that they would choose them as companions on a desert island.

Many of us know people whom we frankly dislike. Our work or social life often throws us together with them. The fact that we do not like them or that they do not like us gives no one the right to make trouble. If we mind our own affairs, there is no trouble.

The objective of parents, then, should be only to set up noncompetitive, independent relationships within the family. Then, as a reward for the elimination of overlapping boundaries, love may bloom.

In summarizing this particular booby trap, we may say that where there is sibling rivalry, all the children are in similar dependency relationships, and the parent must become in, dependent of all of them simultaneously. If and when parents are obliged to interfere, they should not try to be a Solomon-to-the-Judgment and decide which is the "good" child and which is the "bad" child. For close inspection shows that the good one is just as willing to fight as the so-called bad one— and just as capable. The good one selected by the parents maintains a provocative, superior attitude as if he were suffering from halo pressure. He is always on the side of the angels when someone is looking at him. Nor is the bad one as evil as he may appear. The wise parent will believe neither when he finds both upsetting the house with clamor. If they disturb the home so easily, at no cost to themselves, they should be curtailed in their privileges sufficiently to make them realize that they have no right to disturb others. When children know that any fighting in the house results in all parties to the crime losing their allowances or privileges, they cool off quickly enough. If any aggression of one child against another is fundamental, then he will be quite willing to store up his wrath and settle it on the next street corner when he catches the other party in a free position. Such fights, when necessary, may be bitter and decisive; their virtue being that the decisions are made by the children. Moreover, the aggressor has to pay for his victory as much as the other pays for defeat!

It should be remembered that in a family where there is an only child, the problem of jealous competition may arise nevertheless. The first experiences of an only child outside the home may throw him into rivalry with other children. This is apt to happen, because he has not been accustomed to sharing parents, toys, food, or other things on a daily basis inside his home. He has been the favored one and the most loved one by virtue of being the only one. Therefore he may experience shock when it comes time for him to function in the outside world. In school he may find it difficult to accustom himself to the fact that he is not the preferred one or that he must share. If he is not too leaning or dependent on help from others, he will adjust himself to the new situation.

THE FEELING OF REJECTION

Far too much emphasis has been placed on the so-called "rejected child." As a result, many parents assume that if they do not submit to every expectation of a child, he may develop a feeling of rejection. In acceding to every demand made by a child, they believe this will somehow ensure that he will feel secure and loved. To pursue any such course of action is to misguide the child by leading him to believe that his "I want" is a law binding not only on the family but on the community at large. In such a situation, one creates only an extortionist.

Whenever we try to buy good will or love, the price goes up like that of any other commodity. If a child finds that by producing a feeling of rejection, a parent timidly gives in to his every demand, then he makes capital gain out of the feeling of rejection. Each time his parents try to placate him, he has only to raise the price of his forgiveness! And just that much sooner he will find something else to be angry about so that he can collect another unearned dividend of love. When there are a number of such children in a family, there is apt to be constant anger in each of them, so that their parents are continuously obliged to pay tribute to one or the other. What one child gets only acts as a spur for the others to make greater demands. Blackmail can scarcely be a good preparation for life!

It is degrading to bid for the good opinion of others. Children's fundamental needs should be provided impartially, but their wants should never be regarded as more important than the welfare of the family as a whole. It does not hurt a child to become angry and feel rejected if he cannot have his own way at all times. His feelings should be regarded as his own business. He should not be allowed to use them as weapons against those around him.

Far too much attention has been paid to the feelings and emotions of children during these latter years. Far too little attention has been, and is being, paid to keeping the human situation humanly straight in our homes. A child cannot learn too early in life that certain things in life are inescapable, regardless of whether or not he likes them. Feelings, fortunately for all of us, are not laws or reasons for behavior. That is why we keep the Supreme Court busy in the United States. Who would be willing to have justice at the mercy of emotion?

A good example of the principle involved here is found in the Army. Soldiers are told that it is perfectly normal for them to feel afraid, but in spite of such emotions, they are expected to do their full duty in the face of danger. Feelings may not be regarded as reasons. Likewise, no home can be held together properly on any sound basis if parents allow their children's wants (emotions) to control them.

Children very frequently attempt to control and get their own way with tears and fears. Parents should always remember that tears are like hydraulic pressure to wash away opposition. A good antidote for such emotional efforts is matter-of-factness. A parent needs only to state with friendly indifference, when a child tries such tricks, "You may be as angry as you like, for your feelings are your business. But your feelings are no excuse for demanding your own way or for not doing what has to be done."

One of the most sinister aspects of the stress put upon the "rejected" child is the failure to put an equal amount of stress on the fact that a rejected child is in reality also a "rejecting" child. When a child is failing in life, it means that his parents are rejecting him and he is rejecting his parents. The rejection is mutual. It takes two to make a fight. Every stick has two ends. When parents are not gratified by the development of a child, mutual rejection is almost inevitable. The parents feel humiliated and they nag the child to become more like their ideal picture. The child fights back in anger and sabotages the parents. It is a two-way stretch.

To have laid so much stress on the rejected child is to have obscured the fact of mutual rejection. One should never be led astray by thinking of a child as a thing-in-itself. He must be seen as part of his social context. He must keep in mind at all times the whole family portrait and the unique struggle for dominance that goes on within a family. When we do, we find that within a family where rejection exists there has been a mutual process of working at cross-purposes. In such cases, salvation lies distantly. But until things get so far out of control, salvation lies near at hand.

11

WHAT PRICE SALVATION?

Salvation lies near at hand and is obtainable by those parents who truly seek it. Too many parents have been spending too much money in search of magic formulas that they hope will make their children behave better. To them, a half-hundred dollars does not seem too much for a battery of tests that produce some fancy labels, such as "emotionally disturbed child"—which reveals nothing more than they already knew and brings them no nearer salvation. That is because salvation lies in another direction, one that costs a parent nothing more than some willingness to understand and some self-restraint. Actually, all parents have to do is learn to be friends with their children. This means *they must give up their imagined role of superiority and their actual role of inferiority to the child.* To put it even more bluntly, parents have to improve their own behavior if they expect their children's behavior to improve. When parents consider their own welfare as important as the welfare of the child, then it is possible to have fair play in the relationship. In such a case, no child can maintain his persistent and unchallenged infantilism.

This salvation business wouldn't be an issue if parents themselves had more appropriate training before the birth of a child, and understood their parental roles better. When a child is born, it is the mother's job to win its interest. Then she should spread this interest to the father, the child's brothers and sisters, and the community at large. If a mother withdraws a bit of her attention and support each day, the child will have an impetus to try to help himself. At the same time, he will discover the greater satisfaction that will come to him when he does things for himself, and he will gain confidence in his own ability to master the world around him.

The first job of a child is to master the use of the muscles of his arms, legs, and torso and to control his body functions. Overprotected children find no reason to do these things, for too much is done for them. But if a parent wins a bit of freedom each day from his child, the child will master these initial tasks by the age of five or six. Even before then he will not be completely absorbed in himself and he will begin to be interested in other children around him. As this interest grows, he will begin to prefer association with other children to association with his parents and will no longer cling so determinedly to his parents for his emotional and physical satisfactions. Soon he wants to learn to do all the things that other children his age are doing. Almost all of his interest is now centered in the activities of his group, and he comes to regard his parents almost as handicaps or limitations to his freedom.

The child who is developing properly at this age resents the time he must devote to eating, sleeping, and similar things. He finds these functions interfere with his interpersonal relationships with his age-mates. Nor does he want to go visiting with adults on week ends. He is not flattered if his father wants to be his pal, play ball with him, and things of that kind. As one parent put it, "My experience has led me to believe that parents should be free of the awful task of being—God forbid—palsy-walsy with their kids. Then they wouldn't have to give up the editorial page, which is so much more interesting to them than wearing themselves out being a kid's contemporary. It's enough to act kittenish once in a while, but parents shouldn't make a practice of it. Besides, children really don't want a buddy-buddy parent so much as they want somebody at the helm to point out where the shoals and rocks are!" When a child is not obliged to be occupied with schoolwork or his rightful chores, he prefers to be with his friends than with adults, if he is developing properly. Of course, if parents can add to a child's interests and goals without sacrifice to themselves and without enticing the child to become dependent on them, there is no reason why they should exclude themselves.

During this period the growing youngster works out the problems of interpersonal relationships with his peers and learns the lessons of give and take. If nothing interrupts this training period, he finds himself emotionally free from his family by the age of puberty. He has learned to feel at home both in the family and in the world outside. As his sexual interests awaken at puberty, his interest in his pals begins to wane and he becomes attached to someone of the other sex, who begins to interest him more than family or friends. In due time he is ready to begin an independent life with the partner of his choice.

Previously, we have outlined many factors which interrupt this normal development. Nothing that has been written should be misunderstood to mean that our efforts would be directed toward making "obedient" children. The objective is to make self-reliant children. *Children must learn to think and act for themselves in ways that will not interfere with the rights of others around them.* This is not obedience. Obedience is only the feeble-minded child of fear. It is not our objective, as educators, nor should it be the objective of parents, to intimidate children and make them *depend* on us for direction at all times. We should interfere only when children pre-empt our rights or those of others.

There are two kinds of obedience—positive and negative. Neither is preferable to the other. The child who looks to us for our command is seriously crippled in this world. He dares not employ his own initiative and judgment in the solution of his problems. If he depends on others for commands and advice, he will be misled and exploited as a follower who has "no mind of his own."

The right answer to every situation lies within that situation. Each of us should learn to appraise the problem that confronts us and then decide what we think is the most constructive move we can make to improve it. We should not ask others to tell us what to do. Of course, we may misjudge a situation and choose the wrong remedy, for who can be right all the time? But our mistakes should be our own and we should be willing to learn from them. A mistake always should be considered as a friendly invitation to try again!

The obedient person dares not move without command, and he behaves as if he had no authority of his own. Having accepted advice, he blames his failures on the one who misdirected him. A child should be reared so that he understands that he alone must be the author of his failures as well as his successes in life; he must not blame others for what is his doing.

Positive obedience is easily recognized. Negative obedience is much more common than positive obedience but not so readily recognized. It is an even more abject kind of enslavement. Unfortunately, it is always regarded by the child, and frequently by adults, as "independence." In reality, it is only contrariness. The person does just the opposite of what is demanded of him in a situation. It becomes a point of prestige to be in opposition to those around him. He *scorns* the slightest show of obedience and ends up completely obedient in reverse. Delinquent children are usually pure examples of this type of abject obedience. A child in negative obedience may look at a situation and know what he wants out of it, but if his parents suggest the same thing, he will reject it. His whole purpose is to defeat and to dominate the authority figure. As a result, he *has no mind of his own, for he is compelled to do the opposite.* We are reminded of Stella, who had no mind of her own. Her mother asked her whether she would like to have something to drink with lunch. Stella was heard to mutter under her breath, "If she says milk, I shall say cocoa, and if she says cocoa, I shall say milk!" It is not only children who behave in this way. They tell the story in a small Vermont community about the farmer who had been sitting and talking all afternoon on the cracker barrel in the local general store. When it came milking time, he got off the barrel, stretched, and prepared to go home. His parting shot was, "Well, I'm goin' home and have a fight with my wife. If she's milked the cow, it'll be about that. And if she hasn't milked the cow, it'll be about that!"

Whether a child is positively or negatively obedient, he is still in the same situation. He must have a crutch on which to lean. Both types must have someone to tell them what to do, for neither has dared to look at the confronting situation and *act* according to his *own best judgment.* Such children become the tools of the unscrupulous, for they can be led by anyone who will do their thinking for them.

When a parent fails to train a child to act independently for his own welfare and that of others, the child resembles a hypnotic subject. He has no freedom and he lives a life of jealousy. The whole evil of jealousy stems directly from the fact that we become obedient to the one of whom we are jealous. And we are controlled by the acts of the one we hate and envy! He has the initiative, and we become his zombie.

It is like "monkey see, monkey do." Every force of positive and negative obedience comes into play. We cannot employ our own initiative and judgment while we have a feeling of subservience to, and jealousy of, another.

It is mainly for this reason that it is so important for parents to help their children to have minds of their own and not lose them in competitive rivalry wherein each is controlled by the other. In a family situation, if parents are aware of the need for children to develop independence, and refuse to tolerate mutual interference among the children, then children are free to grow up without constantly watching one another. If children are encouraged to think and act independently for themselves when they are young, they will not easily be misled by others when they are adults.

Parents act mistakenly when they insist that children in the family must play together. Contentment depends on each being usefully occupied with his own affairs. When children are not distracted by competition against those around them, they are free to find happiness in pursuing their own "genius." Every child brings into this world his own unique inner demands. These lead him to become interested in certain aspects of the world around him, through which he can express himself. Some like to "see." Some like the feeling of movement. Some like the sound of "sound." Some are delighted by the sense of smell. Each selects one of the senses as his chief interest. His innate genius somehow is built around this faculty, while the other senses are used to support the preferred sense path.

Those who like movement invented airplanes and perfected our transportation systems and traffic control, became athletes, truck drivers, dancers, and engaged in other activities that depend on an interest in and enjoyment of physical movement. Those who like to "see" developed the countless visual activities that depend on the artistic sense. Most of the sciences grew out of the work of those who want to see more deeply into the unknown. From this deep urge we have astronomy, the microscope, atomic research, philosophy, psychology, and every other pursuit of those areas of knowledge in which we try to peer into the darkness of the unknown.

Those who have a genius (curiosity) for sound have given us music, poetry, language, and that whole beautiful world that depends on the ear. Those who delight in the sense of smell have made cooking an art. They have captured the fragrance of the flowers, developed some of the smelliest cheeses, and otherwise made living delightful. They become coffee and tea tasters who control the quality of these products, on which we depend for consolation.

The creative urge lies within each child. It will assert itself when the child is free to shut out the clamor that goes on around him. The so-called "untalented" child is only a child who has been distracted into paying attention only to the rivalries around him and has not been free to listen to the voice or the promptings from within himself. He is caught in a web of competitive jealousy.

Thereafter, his soul stuff is spent in envying anyone who does something better than he and who gets more acclaim. He watches and envies (hates). While he secretly and desperately wishes he could do and have the same, he *pretends to scorn*. However, he believes that the one who does something better is some kind of authority and that any puny efforts he himself might make would not win approval. He believes that even if he tried, he would be laughed at and ridiculed. These mistaken beliefs lead him to move away from that area. He does not try to train in that area because his competitive jealousy is too great and he thinks his only success in any area lies in surpassing others. Since he doesn't try, he gains no skill. So he sits with his jealousy. His hurt feelings are uppermost in his mind. Fear of failure has stopped him in his tracks. This, of course, should be viewed as an expression of hostility on his part toward others around him. He is caught on the horns of the dilemma of obedience to authority on one side and dependence on the opinion of others on the other. We can understand this dilemma best if we define it as "chasing two rabbits at once." This is the stuff of which all the so-called "emotional blocks" are made. Most, if not all, children being labeled "mentally retarded" are in this category, too. There is nothing wrong with their mental capacity. It is being used to chase the wrong rabbit!

To attempt to chase two rabbits at once, both going in opposite directions, is to lose both. Parents who really love their children see to it that they are not enslaved into fighting with those around them, so that they are free to respond to their own inner urges, to develop them, to explore them. Then a child is prepared to be his own master.

With no jealousies to occupy his thoughts and feelings, a child pays attention to the call of these promptings of his genius. He is not so tied down by fear of failure that he does not dare expose himself to experiences in these areas. He isn't afraid of being ridiculed. His genius grows as he feeds it with experiences, and in time he shows his natural aptitude in his own direction. He then begins his conscious training to perfect these inner trends. By the time he is grown he has chosen the area in which he wants to make his contribution to society. He has chosen his vocation.

When parents so train their children, they allow them to keep their birthrights!

12

THE BIG TENT AND
THE LITTLE SIDE SHOW

Every circus has its little side show. Its main tent has at least three rings, and many performers do their separate jobs simultaneously. Not one of these performers expects that the eyes of the audience will be on him or her alone. At all times, some death-defying spectacle is going on in every part of the main tent. The spectators may choose to watch whatever interests them most. This vast and varied spectacle is made up of individual acts capable of working independently without reference to one another.

Side shows, however, are built on a different principle. There is usually one performer. All eyes are turned toward him in the middle of his little tent. He holds his position in the side show on the basis of some "gimmick" entirely his own. His act is such that it might be overlooked in the main tent because it is too intricate, too revolting, or has to be seen close up if it is to be seen at all. For example, physically deformed people sometimes display themselves and thereby capitalize on their deformities. They make their living by exciting pity and stimulating our morbid curiosities, instead of engaging in a productive occupation elsewhere.

This is a good analogy for us to use in order to understand the differences in the roles played by a child who is growing up to be self-sufficient and the so-called problem child. The former does his job independently, with a minimum of help, whether or not anyone is watching him. He does not disrupt others in the Main Tent who are doing their jobs. These children share the tent with other co-workers. They do not have to depend on something bizarre or revolting as a device to attract attention to themselves. Usually their act demands more training than that of a Side-Show performance.

The problem child, however, has chosen to perform in Side-Show activities because he is not prepared adequately to perform in the Main Tent, where he would really prefer to be. That is his little secret. Although he may pretend no interest in the Main Tent, he is envious of the ability he sees there—all the while hiding this fact. He manages to do this by finding some bizarre "gimmick" that will distract his audience from the Main Tent and will conceal the fact that he is not performing in the larger arenas of life.

One of the most difficult things to explain to parents is why a child bites his nails, wets his bed, has night terrors, tics, or any of the other countless manifestations of maladjustment. Many parents find it difficult to understand, for instance, how a child can gain anything from sleeping in a wet bed. More than that, these same parents rarely see any relationship between a child's Side-show activities at home (such as nail-biting or bed-wetting) and his academic or behavior failures at school. They do not like to accept the fact that at school, as well as at home, the child has wooed his audience into his Side Show and thereby has distracted attention from his failure to perform in the Main Tent!

Countless children are brought to guidance clinics for treatment of tics and other unsightly symptoms that irritate the parents. If these symptoms were not so annoying to the parents, they would not have bothered to seek help for the child at all. Although this same child has been failing or doing poorly in school for years, they think that is only because he is "not very bright." They fail to see the least common denominator that relates both things. The tic and the school deficiency are both equally valuable to the child as ways to center the attention of the audience on him. They do not understand that his whole scheme of life depends on keeping everyone dancing attendance on him. Without this gimmick to tie his audience to him, he would have to learn to get along on his own.

It would be well if everyone could understand why it is that these behavior problem children represent a sort of hash, with all kinds of assorted, troublesome, annoying manifestations mixed together. Such children manage to be almost constantly disquieting or burdensome, regardless of where they may be. If they are squelched in one way of attracting notice or help, they quickly find another. The final result is that the adults around the child spend most of their time watching his Side-show activities and have little time for their own performance in the Main Tent. They get so bogged down and so mystified in the Side Show that they lose sight of their own target, which is to teach the child to be independent and to be independent themselves. If they concentrated on their own target, they would not be turning their heads constantly in this child's direction, and he would be cheated out of his illegal gains.

No effort should be made to cure any one symptom. To try to do so is to focus attention just where the child wants everyone to keep looking. The child who stammers, for example, has everyone around him finishing the sentences he begins. This is a fine way of getting attention. Or else they scold him, which is just as effective for his purposes, since it, too, is a sign of attention. He cannot give up stammering until he becomes more independent. If he becomes more independent he will not need to stammer when confronted by life problems. But until then the Main Tent will remain neglected, because as long as people tarry in his speech Side Show they forget the tasks that he should be undertaking. For example, he will probably be excused from oral recitation in school, or be free to use his stammering as an excuse for not going to the grocery store for his mother, "because he cannot give the order when he gets there." The only way to avoid getting caught in Side Shows is to talk about something else when children try to capture us with their gimmick. We must not accept their excuses for what they "can't do" at such times. On the contrary, that is the time to give them a job they can do, and then see to it that it gets done before any privilege is granted.

This is best illustrated by a story about a six-year-old boy called Eddie who was invited to drive into the country with his uncle and aunt, who had hired a horse and buggy for the trip. While driving along a country road, a newspaper blew toward the horse. The horse started to rear up in the traces and was about to bolt in panic. Eddie's uncle flayed the horse with the buggy whip until it stopped its antics and broke into a run. It passed the paper on the road without noticing it. At this point the horse was more interested in its smarting flank. The uncle was soon able to pull the horse down to a walk and the excitement was ended.

Eddie, however, was aghast. His uncle had always been the soul of kindness, and Eddie could not understand his apparently savage behavior in beating the frightened horse. He began to remonstrate with his uncle. The uncle was not at a loss to explain. "Remember this, my boy: horses are much like people. They often get scared of things they don't understand. That is dangerous. Whenever you drive a horse and he gets scared of something he doesn't understand, just give him the whip because that is something he does understand. That will take his mind off his imaginary troubles."

In relating this story we are not inferring that parents have to use a buggy whip. But parents should find ways to divert their own attention and that of the child from his symptomatic behavior. They should keep his attention, and their own, on the job that remains to be done by him. No good comes from devoting anxious care to symptoms in themselves. To do so is like putting a hot iron on a wrinkle and pressing it in deeper. The more a parent nags a child about facial grimaces, thumb-sucking, stammering, and similar things, the more stubbornly do they fasten their own attention and that of the child on the very weapon he is using so successfully to annoy them. The molehill becomes a mountain and blots out recognition of the failure in the Main Tent.

The important thing for parents to remember about Sideshow performances is that they are substitute activities that the child has inadvertently discovered to be useful for filling up his time, instead of devoting his attention to performing in the Main Tent, which he believes is hopelessly beyond him.

The child is discouraged about gaining any success by legitimate efforts in the Main Tent. Were we able to take away from him the attention and significance he wins by his symptoms, his feelings of worthlessness would sweep over him like a flood. No one can live without some feelings of significance, even if they are based only on making trouble for, and obsessing, others. This is why a little boy who wants to make a big impression on a pretty little girl will sometimes eat a woolly worm while she is watching, if only to make her scream. He etches the memory of himself on her, and she will not forget him all her life, even though she may not grow to like him as he wanted her to do. Had he known how to win her approval by some constructive action, he would not have been reduced to eating the worm, which was as repugnant to him as to her.

Another reason for not treating a single symptom, per se, is that if we took away one irritating symptom, the child would only substitute another in its place. Getting rid of symptoms is a negative approach and would still leave the child with *no training to succeed in the Main Tent.* He would not have overcome his inabilities and his fears. However, if we focus our efforts toward success in the area from which he has been fleeing, he will eventually find the knack of doing the job. Then seven wild horses cannot keep him back, and he will drop his symptoms *because he no longer has any need for them.*

Vivian dropped her symptoms when efforts were finally focused on keeping her in the area from which she kept running so cleverly. Her main symptoms were fears and tears— at least, these were the two symptoms that most irritated her mother and teacher. When Vivian was six she started school, leaving behind at home a new baby sister. Almost immediately Vivian began to develop fears. She complained that in school they took her to the basement where it was dark, and the teacher had to hold her hand. Already we can see that Vivian manged to use her fears to get her teacher into her Side Show. That isn't the only symptom she used to trap her teacher, as we shall see.

Very shortly after starting school, Vivian had a cold that kept her at home for three weeks. While home, she continued to observe how attentive her mother was to her baby sister. When she returned to school the children in her class had progressed. So here, too, she felt put back. She began to cry at school. She upset the teacher, who mistook her tears for weakness or ill health. Every morning her mother took her to school, but by the time the mother returned home, the telephone would be ringing. She would be asked to come back to school and get Vivian, who had cried every single moment since she had left. The teacher would suggest that perhaps Vivian would like to return later in the day. But once Vivian was back home, that ended school for the day. She didn't refuse outright to return for the afternoon session, but she would say to her mother, "I will go tomorrow." And she would. However, the crying routine would be repeated. Thus Vivian managed each day to escape activities in the Main Tent.

During the day at home, Vivian stayed close by her baby sister's crib. Sometimes she would play with toys or draw, but she would never let her mother out of sight. At three o'clock she would go out to play with the children in the neighborhood when they returned from school. But from morning until three in the afternoon she kept her mother busy in her Side Show. She whined and fussed. She shouted and slapped. She had temper outbursts about the simplest things. Her mother would try to reason with her, but Vivian's logic always succeeded in defeating the mother. Vivian somehow managed to get her own way all the time. For instance, she would ape the baby, demanding to be fed as the baby was.

Vivian's mother was distraught. Finally she sought guidance. The Big Tent and Little Side Show business was explained. She was advised that it was necessary for this child to face life more realistically and that she herself must not be so easily subordinated by Vivian. A plan was presented to the mother and she was asked to win the teacher's cooperation. The plan was that she was to take Vivian to school with a large man's handkerchief pinned to her dress. The teacher was to arrange a special "crying corner" behind a screen. Vivian was to be told that she might cry as much as she liked in the future, but that she must do it in her private crying corner so as not to disturb the class. Mother was not to be called by the teacher. Vivian was to remain in school.

As soon as Vivian arrived in school the next morning she promptly turned on the water power, as she had been doing in the past. The new plan was put into operation that very day. The teacher ushered her to the corner and gave her a most gracious permission to cry to her little heart's content. Then the class went on as if nothing had happened. Vivian soon became bored with her corner, her handkerchief, and her tears. She was smart enough to realize that a halt had been called on her being superintendent of both the school and the home. There was nothing left for her to do but join her classmates. So she did. After that she went to school minus handkerchief and minus tears. She began to enjoy school and to get into the thick of things.

Vivian's story illustrates that the way to get someone out of a Side Show is to take the profit out of it. A Side-show activity is always a form of infantile behavior. The more parents urge a child to give up his infantile symptoms, the tighter he clings to them. The child knows he is holding on to his parents, and that's what he wants to do! When parents view the picture of symptoms correctly, then they can change their whole strategy. In other words, the trick is to put the shoe on the other foot and walk away!

We might make a comparison here by describing two different ways of handling a typical trick children use to entice a parent into a Side Show. Let us say that it is a rainy afternoon. Junior cannot go out to play. A Captive Mother would handle the situation one way. An Independent Mother would handle it another.

Our Captive Mother is busy with household tasks when Junior interrupts her, whining, "What can I do? It's raining outside."—as if she didn't know it. "Why don't you play with that Erector set you begged us to buy you?" she asks. He responds, "I don't want to play with the Erector set." Hopefully, his mother says, "Then play with your toy soldiers." "Aw, that's no fun alone," Junior says. "Well, then," the mother suggests wearily, "what about using your new paint set that you insisted we get for you?" "No," Junior storms, "I'm not going to mess around with any ole paints today." As his mother turns off the oven and scrubs the dough off her hands, she says, "Well, would you like Mother to read to you?" She has known all along that's the answer he has been waiting for, so finally she capitulates.

Now, let us see what would happen with Independent Mother on such a day. When Junior disrupts her chores with his whines about what to do, she says in a friendly, though indifferent, tone of voice, "Well, I'm sure I don't know what you should do to amuse yourself. You must figure that out yourself. It really isn't my problem. My problem is this work I have to do. Perhaps you would enjoy helping me with my chores. Here is a dust rag. How would you like to dust the living room?" It has even been known to happen that Junior picked up the rag and helped Mother. But probably Independent Mother won't hear any more from Junior for some hours! If she goes to look for him, she will find him happily engaged doing something of his own choosing that magically appeared as soon as he found he could not pin her down into being an unpaid entertainer for the afternoon.

These two illustrations of the way in which two different mothers might handle the same situation produce two different results. One mother wastes her time in slavery, while her job goes a-beggin'. The other mother keeps her independence and gets her job done. In the first illustration, mother and son *together add up to less than one.* Neither uses his own capacities for his own development. By just that much, each is more dependent on the other. In the second illustration, mother and son have a chance to develop their own inner resources and to discover some application of their own creative instincts. Both are in a more independent position, for this approach *grants to each his own center of gravity and produces self-sufficiency.*

Common sense tells us that no child beyond the infancy stage is so weak that he cannot amuse himself. A parent doesn't get dragged away from the Main Tent into a Side Show unless he believes in the myth of a Weak Character!

13

WHO'S A WEAK CHARACTER?

Many parents have been led astray by believing that their child has a weak will—just as many a thirsty man has died in the desert, following a mirage that appeared to be an oasis. When parents delude themselves in this fashion they become hopelessly trapped and bogged down in futile efforts to strengthen the child's weak will.

Parents cannot get on with the job of training their children properly unless they have a clear picture of this thing called a weak will. They should learn to differentiate quickly between real weakness and what only looks like weakness. A rattrap is entirely passive—until the victim ventures into it. Then it snaps shut with implacable resolution. Flypaper is entirely passive. A fly is lost, however, once he lights on it. Every move he makes to push it away from him only fastens him more tightly to it. Mud is the quietest kind of material. However, the strongest automobile may find itself powerless to move in it. The more its wheels spin, the deeper it bogs down. The same is true of quicksand!

In addition to passivity, there is a long list of behavior difficulties that are often mentioned as evidence of a weak character. Some of these are overeating, nail-biting, thumb-sucking, daydreaming, whining, crying, lack of concentration, laziness, lethargy, forgetfulness, lying, cheating, and stealing.

Parents can never understand the meaning of such character traits unless they are able to see how these traits cut down the demands they make on the child. These are ways the child finds to make life easier for himself and harder for those around him. The child, of course, does not plan consciously any of these tricks. But if he did do it consciously, he could not come up with better answers than the ones he has found by trial and error as he goes along. Weakness is a genuine lack of power to meet a situation in a direct manner, of course. But this does not mean that a child cannot and will not use it as one of the strongest weapons to conquer his opposition. How does a child discover how to use the power hidden in *appearing* weak? A child is like a general who is always on the watch for some strategy that will lead the opposition to exhaust its forces without gaining any permanent advantage.

What general, in any war, would tell the enemy where his lines are weakest? And yet this is exactly what many parents do! If they have a child whom they consider a "weak character," they are given to expounding long and loud on his sins. It is as though they said, "These are the points where you get under my skin." In so doing, parents only point out their own weak spots. The child might not think of so many strategies to exhaust his parents if they were not called to his attention constantly in such recitals. Thus all the nagging that parents do only serves the child's purposes. They might as well hand the child a gun and then point at their hearts and beg to be shot!

If parents have been trapped in the hopeless effort to strengthen a Little Weak Character in this way, what can they do to help themselves? First, they must realize that the old frontal attack they have been using has been their downfall. They should first view this business as if it were a game of tug of war into which they have been drafted unwittingly. Then they will see that the only quick and effective answer is to let go their end of the rope and go on about their own business! Their Weak Character will fall down, of course. They should let him lie there as they disappear into the distance. He will not lie there long before he gets on his feet and comes running after them. Since such a child is a dependent, leaning type who is not yet ready to stand independently, he can be counted on to scramble after his parents.

Here is a story about six-year-old Harold, who was such a Weak Character. Harold's parents took some friends on a picnic to the seashore. The father and one of his friends decided to walk along the beach. Harold insisted on accompanying them, against the wishes of his father. Harold won the battle, as he was accustomed to do. He kept trailing about five hundred yards behind all the while. Every few minutes his father would remember to look for him. He would yell, "Hurry up, Harold, and catch up to us." Then he would keep his friend waiting until Harold did catch up. This finally became a great irritation. The father decided to spank this lagging son of his, but his friend suggested a better strategy. He said, "Let's choose a comfortable pace for ourselves and walk along as if we were alone on the beach. And let's not look back to see what Harold is doing." This was an agreeable suggestion because the game of tug of war had become so irritating to Harold's father.

And so they walked along as if they had not been accompanied by Weak Character. Almost immediately, Harold sensed a change in the situation. He began yelling, "Daddy, Daddy, wait for me, wait for me." But his father pretended to be deaf. Within no time, the panting Harold had caught up with his father and his friend. For the remainder of the walk he was ten paces ahead of them the entire time. This story proves the old adage: "If you can't lick 'em, then join 'em!"

There is certainly such a thing as being in a weak or a poor situation. Many children find themselves in such a situation. But their human wills soon find a way to handle it, even if that way is to climb upon someone's back and stay there as long as they find it profitable. For instance, Fred was like that. He was eight. No one was able to get Fred off their backs because everyone thought he was weak. His parents believed he was, and so did the school.

Fred was the younger of two children. He used his weakness to control his father, his mother, and his older sister. He managed in the same way to control his teacher. At home, he kissed his mother endlessly. He cried for every little thing. He had always cried—that is, from the time he discovered that this strategy washed away opposition. He learned to use his fears in the same way; thus he dominated his adult trainers. They were in his power, for he saw to it that they were constantly occupied with his petulance, his wants, and his demands.

There were many manifestations of Fred's power techniques at home. For instance, he was rigid to exasperation. He would not change his way of doing anything—ever. He became furious and threw temper tantrums if things did not go the way he wanted them to. He had his own hour to watch television unmolested—whatever program he wished to watch. However, he insisted on dictating to the family just what program they were to watch during the hour that was supposed to be theirs exclusively.

Fred kept the whole family in turmoil each mealtime. He criticized the food that was put on the table. If he decided the food wasn't the right color or that "it stank," he insisted that no one else eat it, either. He worried and fussed endlessly about inconsequentials. It was the family's custom on Sundays to celebrate by eating out. But Fred succeeded in ruining each Sunday dinner for the rest of the family by carping and nagging from the moment they left the front door, and all the while they were in the restaurant, that he wouldn't get back home in time to watch his favorite television program at five o'clock.

In school he used passivity, inattention, tears, and apparent helplessness to control his teacher. He frustrated her in as many ways as he did his family. Thus Fred managed to use weakness as a powerful weapon to subdue all the supposedly stronger ones around him. There would not be so many Freds if adults didn't habitually view children as weak because they are small. When adults do this they misread all the signs of will and determination that these children display. The total behavior of such children has to be read as disruptive and disjunctive. Behavior is always either a movement "toward" or a movement "away from" cooperation.

The position in which all adults who deal with Fred-types find themselves is like the two men who went out one night to hunt raccoons. One flashed the light into the tree while the other climbed out on a limb of the tree to bag the game. They saw two eyes reflecting light. The climber crawled along the limb to make the catch. Then came a surprising commotion in the dark. The fellow on the ground called up, "Hang on till I come up and help to hold him." His friend in the tree screamed back, "Hold him! This is a wildcat. I need someone to turn me loose!"

No adult would lose his way if he understood and remembered at all times that in these children he faces a human will as strong as his own. Parents should never forget this point. For they, above all others, have experienced the will of the newborn infant! From the moment of birth an infant's will exercises as much force in the family as the oldest adult.

This difficulty in misreading the evidence can be avoided when the labels are changed. What has been regarded as weakness of will must be labeled persisting infantilism. In other words, individuals who have been thought of as weak should be thought of as people who are using infantile behavior as a weapon for gaining and holding dominance. Why should a person select weapons from the nursery? The answer is simple. The actual weakness of the newborn infant moves all society to serve it day and night. Anyone, regardless of age, who wants to remain king is tempted to use childish behavior. There is no other technique so compelling as that of remaining dead weight in order to be carried around by others!

II

THE SCHOOL PORTRAIT or
STUPIDITY AS AN EXEMPTION

14

WHO'S RETARDED?

School is the first important job given a child to do outside the home. The entire course of his life may be influenced by the success or failure of this first step toward the future. Any child who is not born organically feeble-minded can succeed in school if we prepare him properly for the job before he begins it. And it is our task to make sure that he does not fail. If we do not fail in our preparation of the child, he will be able to meet the demands which this new situation puts upon him.

Those of us who have lived with children know that those who fall behind in school lose courage. For those who walk without courage, there looms a life path of mediocrity and nonfulfillment. Penologists tell us that the majority of inmates in our jails are individuals who did not do well in school and did not learn a useful occupation. Our mental institutions are filled with those who never had the courage to accept reality and never learned how to get along with their fellow men.

Before the invention of intelligence tests, it was assumed that children who failed in school did so because they lacked the capacity to learn. These tests, however, show that there is no direct relationship between the intelligence score and adequate school performance. Many with high scores fail badly, and some with relatively low scores manage to do the work. When this became apparent, it was assumed that some kind of special gift was needed for certain subjects and that one might be competent in most areas but still lack the "gift" of mathematics, spelling, or reading. And we might be tempted to believe this if experience did not show that many such individuals suddenly found themselves operating capably in areas where we had been assured nothing could or would develop. Very often they became especially competent in the area in which they had been the weakest or slowest in getting started.

There is not now, as there once was, such widespread and blind faith in mental tests. Many have surrendered the notion that they are a final statement about the mental capacity of an individual. However, in too many quarters this faith remains unshaken to this day. There is no way to evaluate the damage that has resulted and is still resulting from a blind acceptance of these test results. Countless children have been labeled "mentally retarded" and then ignored as being unteachable. This tragedy has blighted the whole future of unnumbered armies of children.

We must ask ourselves whether it is our children who are "mentally retarded." History may record that it was we, not they, who were the stupid ones—a case of the blind leading the blind! It may even describe the widespread use of, and uncritical faith in, the I.Q. as one of the greatest disasters of the twentieth century. Ruth Benedict, a famous anthropologist, wrote in her *Patterns of Culture*:

"The Puritan Divines of New England, in the 18th Century, were the last persons whom contemporary opinion in the Colonies regarded as psychopaths. Few prestige groups have been allowed such complete intellectual and emotional dictatorship as they were. They were the Voice of

God. Yet to a modern observer, it is they, not the confused and tormented women they put to death as witches, who were the psychoneurotics of Puritan New England. . . ."

The social anthropologists of the future, writing about psychologists of today, may record that they behaved much like the Puritan Divines of the eighteenth century in believing that they were the Voice of God whose numerical brain ratings were reality.

It is to the credit of some teachers that, with greater experience and insight, they have tended to become more mellow in their judgments in this respect. They now tend to accept present level of functioning rather than to assert that the test score represents fundamental capacities of an individual. This has made a crack in the wall of our ineptness. It will be a happy day when all of us accept the fact that no child should be judged by static test results that purport to measure the length, breadth, and weight of what is inside a child's head.

In historical perspective, mankind has always divided itself into two groups: those who are sure a thing cannot be done, and those who are determined to find a way to do everything and anything. When the locomotive was invented, many were certain that high speeds would kill people. They said, "God did not intend man to go fast." But the optimists kept working, and now we fly faster than the speed of sound. As teachers of our children, we should remain on the side of those who are determined to do the *impossible*, for that is the direction of life and of evolution. We are free to choose whether we shall regard the I.Q. as a tombstone over the future of a child or whether we shall regard it as merely a glance in a mirror as we travel toward future goals.

The most a test can tell us is something about the child's present ability to pass the test. A child sometimes fails a test because he becomes nervous and confused, even though he may know the material well enough. Failure may not indicate incapacity as much as lack of confidence under stress. How often have we forgotten the name of an old friend at the moment we began to introduce him to a stranger? Would we want that to stand as a final score of our intelligence?

We should remember that intelligence is not the *private affair* of an individual, any more than is the language he speaks. Intelligence, like language, is a social factor. Intelligence is a human capacity that developed, along with our other faculties, out of the interdependence of human beings. It is an inborn potentiality that is stiumulated by the human way of living and is generated within a social context. It is a kind of instrument we perfect in the struggle for survival.

This viewpoint usually brings forth cries of anguish from those who choose to believe each of us is born with a fixed and unalterable amount of intelligence. The dispute between those who like to believe we create our own intelligence and those who like to believe it is a special gift to the individual can never be settled with finality. But it seems more reasonable to believe that intelligence is a product of social evolution, along with all our other inborn human potentialities, each of which waits for our needs and our interest to waken them into fulfillment, than to believe that intelligence is foreordained or predetermined. It is the magic touch of keen interest that brings intelligence into action.

Let us for a moment accept the proposition that all human beings have every human potentiality inherent in them at birth. In other words, what any man has done, all can do to a degree. The word "degree," in this instance, refers to "degree of competence." How high this degree will be depends largely on how great an interest a person has in training his potential. Many imponderables in the life of an individual affect his interest and the energy he brings to his training.

Surely it is most improbable that any test will ever be devised that can tell us the exact amount of past training, energy, and interest (willingness) a person brings to a test. If the test result is high, it can mean only that the person brought a good amount of each to the test. If the test result is low, it can tell us only what we should know already—that we, as educators, must strive harder to find a way to improve the activity and interest of the person tested.

Let us take pause here and consider Johnny, who is six, in the light of the above concepts. Here is a child who, from the beginning of his life, has been pampered and overprotected. He has had no training in self-reliance or self-sufficiency. Johnny is a leaning, dependent individual. He has a mistaken map of the world that reads, "Life is a something-for-nothing business." When he started going to school he left behind in his mother's arms a newborn brother. For Johnny, going to school represented leaving the fort (home) in command of the enemy. Until recently Mother has been his crutch, and his crutch is now at home with the baby. So from the very beginning Johnny rejects school. His body is there, but his mind is not free to interest itself in other children or in school achievement. His mind and soul are consumed with jealousy. This jealousy leads him to "out-baby the baby" while at home, as a means of holding on to his parents' attention. In school he finds that at first his apparent helplessness brings him extra-special attention. But he has placed himself, without awareness, in double jeopardy. His parents, who do not understand why he acts so silly, resent his persisting infantilism and reject his behavior. And in school he is cut off from full participation because his classmates, meanwhile, have progressed, and they find him a stumbling block in their path. He has no idea that all this has happened because he has rejected his environment, which he can no longer have on his own terms. On the contrary, he believes that everyone has rejected him. Poor Johnny! Eventually he will be tested and may be labeled "mentally retarded"!

When a child becomes angry and rejects his environment, it causes him to create social-distance and feeling-distance between himself and those around him. He does not call fully upon his basic capacities while he is at a feeling-distance from his society. Why should we be surprised that he does not develop latent capacities into manifest abilities? Why should we judge a child who has not been trained to feel equal to the life around him on the same terms as a child who has been trained for self-reliance and to do his share in life?

No test has yet been invented that will judge the imponderables of human beings. It helps us in no way, in the education of children, to regard their I.Q. as a limit on their future achievements set by fate or heredity. Neither the child nor the parent should know his I.Q. because they may regard it as a final judgment of his limitations. Thus the child or parent may give up trying to find new ways for stimulating the desired development. All education is, in the end, self-education. The greatest difficulty we face in self-education is what we ourselves imagine to be our limitations. If we have prematurely decided that success is beyond us, we become hopeless and explore no further.

The main task of education should be to increase the courage and the interest of each individual so that he will not set arbitrary limits on his own inherent powers. "Love laughs at locksmiths," the old saying goes. If we love anything deeply enough, we will find a way to unlock the riddle in its heart! Nothing can hold us back as long as our interest burns hotly.

The really limiting disadvantage of the intelligence quotient is that it does not tell us how to help the failing child. It gives us no hint as to how to get the child with the high I.Q. to apply his unquestioned intelligence toward useful achievements. And it cries aloud the apparent hopelessness of doing anything for the child with the low score. What does it profit us to use such tests when faced with a child who is not growing properly toward a position of usefulness in society? We have the same problem in either case. We must find a way, quite independently of an intelligence score, to help the child. It has done unquestioned harm in the past and, as we shall see, is of no great help even in prognosis.

Many years ago intelligence tests were given to a group of school children and the records were kept. Years elapsed. Then these same individuals, now grown up and working in various communities, were surveyed to see whether they had achieved according to their I.Q.s, measured so many years before. There was found to be no correlation at all between past record and recent performance! Few of those with the highest scores had done anything of note. Most of them were quite undistinguished. But some of those with scores that had been considered borderline and next to feeble-minded were found to be the heads of successful businesses, leaders in the community in different ways, and valued citizens to whom others turned for help or guidance.

In an experiment at the Hawthorne plant of the Western Electric Company, studies of a group of workers were made, using tests of manual dexterity and intelligence. Then their actual production in the plant was measured. Again, no correlation was found between their I.Q. and dexterity scores and their productivity on the job. One of the smartest (I.Q.-wise) did the least work on the job. Perhaps that was proof of his intelligence! Who can say?

Who is truly wise enough to know the limits of human capacity? For the practical purposes of education, at least, we should consider all children who are not constitutionally feeble-minded as educatable. It is a show of arrogance on our part, as well as a criminal injustice against the child, for us to use any approach to training other than one of unlimited optimism.

Courage is contagious, and so is pessimism. We should adopt no opinions that fasten the pessimism of our views on that wonderfully resourceful invention of evolution—the human child. Let us start now to assume joyously that any child can learn to do anything that other children are able to do in our schoolrooms. Let us no longer quibble over the limits of human intelligence. Rather, let us agree together, here and now, that no test can ever plumb the depths of a child's mind or soul nor predict his future. If we are ignorant and mistaken in this viewpoint, we can damage no one by holding it. The courage we derive from it is more productive than the results of pessimism. The sublime ignorance of optimism alone can accomplish the impossible! We learned to fly without growing wings, didn't we?

15

IS IT ALL TRUE–
WHAT THEY SAY ABOUT
FEEBLE-MINDEDNESS?

They said he was feeble-minded. We refer, now, to Richard.
He arrived at a reform school at seventeen. Previously, he had
flunked every intelligence test, every achievement test, and
every subject in school. This only proves that his teachers had
done no better job than his parents in reconciling him to his
environment and in initiating him into the fellowship of
mankind.

Nor were administrators of this institution for delinquents
any wiser than his parents and teachers. Richard confronted
them with his erratic behavior. It was easier for them to hide
behind a belief in some imagined intellectual impairment
than to consider ways of winning his cooperation. They sent
him to a clinic to be retested. The clinic hung a "tombstone
of feeble-mindedness" around his neck for him to carry to his
future grave.

On his return from the clinic, Richard, in a voice of lofty
scorn, discussed the experience at the clinic with a counselor
who had been wise enough to win his trust. "Do you know
what that dumb psychologist did?" asked Richard. "He
showed me a picture of a man sawing wood with the saw up-

side down and asked me whether I could see anything wrong in the picture!" When his friend the counselor inquired what response he had made, he answered, "I told him, 'Naw, it looks all right to me.'" (*Any psychometrist who believes that a child with no training in cooperation either can or will cooperate with him and his test material has delusions that need investigation.*)

And yet this supposedly feeble-minded boy, in a casual conversation with the counselor, had asked whether light has color, per se, and whether it can be seen! This question led to a long discussion of light, color, and finally to interstellar space. Richard asked penetrating questions that showed he followed explanations, since his questions arose from an understanding of previous answers given to him.

In spite of the lone protest of his counselor friend, Richard, in the eyes of the law and in the view of his teachers, was feeble-minded. That's what they said. He was soon transferred from the school for delinquents to a school for feeble-minded children, there to await the graveyard. Whose was the crime? Whose intelligence was at fault?

This is only one example out of thousands. If we have so little faith in the potentialities of children, why should they have any faith in themselves? From whom shall they learn the courage to keep trying? Children are most sensitive to our attitudes and are the first to detect when we feel a lack of confidence in ourselves and in them. Discouragement prevents us from gathering together our inner powers to overcome limitations. Only courage can give us strength to dare. When a child is faced with our pessimism about his future, we give him an excellent reason for acquiring the semblance of feeble-mindedness. He becomes apathetic, and apathy is the semblance of feeble-mindedness.

True feeble-mindedness is an organic defect arising from imperfect development of the fetus. Multiple indications are apparent, both in the body and the behavior of the individual. The truly feeble-minded child can be recognized without an I.Q. test. Fortunately, feeble-mindedness is rather rare. The retardation of such children is so marked, in so many ways, that they are seldom sent to school in the first place. They do not develop rudimentary common sense. They are medical problems for hospital care. They are not the children of whom we speak.

We speak of, and are concerned with, the increasing body of children who learn quickly those things we do not want them to know and show an amazing resistance to learning most of the things we want them to master. We believe that any child can meet the minimum demands of school, granted he is not truly feeble-minded. Schools expect so little nowadays that all children can do what is required if their minds are on the job. But there's the rub! Any child who can follow the intricate plot of a radio or television drama, and remember it, has the mental capacity to succeed in school.

Let us make the above even more clear. A little girl of six was considered by her pediatrician, the school, and everyone else who had dealt with her to be mentally retarded. She seemed almost helpless when it came to putting on her clothes, combing her hair, lacing her shoes, and other things she might be expected to do at her age. Watching her, one might think her wrists were broken. She spoke endlessly a kind of word salad that closely imitated her mother's conversation but was meaningless. Most of the time she even looked stupid and dull. There was almost nothing to encourage one to believe that she might be intelligent. However, she betrayed a devilish ability to mimic the salient aspects of the behavior of various people who interested her. Her penetrating observation of their foibles equaled anything seen on the Broadway stage. She never failed to pick out the one thing in any situation that was calculated to upset the adult environment, such as repeating tidbits of forbidden gossip, off-color words, and similar gibby-gabby things. Only a child with superior knowledge could abstract the salient elements of a character or a situation with such deadly precision. But it was not until she had been made more self-reliant that her intelligence showed itself on the positive side of life. As originally expressed in conventional tests and observations, she was labeled mentally retarded!

It is a great mistake for teachers or parents to imagine that every child has as his purpose the desire to learn only or any of those things we choose to have him learn. If a child does not pick up quickly the information presented to him by a teacher, he is regarded as being slow in learning. We like to believe that there are differences in the innate ability to learn quickly. We assume a lack of mental capacity on that slender evidence. But whoever said the child wanted to learn the lesson taught him? It is like advising a spendthrift to save his money for his old age. He does not hear us or wish to hear us. This is a flaw of judgment and value system on his part, rather than a lack of mental capacity with which to learn. This same flaw operates in the case of many so-called feeble-minded children.

Another argument given to prove limited mental capacity is that the slow child cannot keep up with the bright child. We might believe this if we saw the slow child toiling as the turtle did in his race against the hare. He might use persistence to compensate for what was lacking in speed. But we see no such thing. We see no desire to toil at all toward the goals we have set for him. On the contrary, we can get him to our chosen goals only by duress, and then we find that his spirit is not with us. We have led the horse to water, only to have to push him into it!

Neither the viewpoint expressed in this book nor the still-current faith in the validity of intelligence tests can be proved with any finality. However, since as the trainers of children we must have a working hypothesis, it would seem preferable to have an optimistic rather than a pessimistic approach to the understanding of children. We tend to see only what we are looking for and avoid seeing that which contradicts us. As Shakespeare said, "Nothing is but thinking makes it so." We approach or retreat from situations according to the meanings we ascribe to them. Pessimism carefully locks all doors without investigating what lies behind them. Without faith in "things not seen," we cannot realize our desires. Who would bother to rear a baby in the first place if he did not have faith in its inherent powers to grow and develop into usefulness? So why give up an optimistic hypothesis in the middle of the stream and decide a child will not develop any further? We reckon without the child when we do this. He does continue to develop and may become our hangman if we fail him. It is to our own advantage to see that he develops into usefulness and not to let despair guide his hand. Neither the child nor ourselves know the outside limits of his potentialities. Why pretend we do?

The only valid test of intelligence, actually, is the ability of a child to achieve a purpose of his own selection, whether that goal be good or bad. He, like all of us, will work only for that which has meaning and value in his eyes, and then only to the degree he believes it to be important to him. We ought never to underestimate the intelligence of a child nor the limits of his capacities. His ability to talk us out of a firm stand we have taken, or his inventive ways of getting out of chores is a better indication of his intelligence than any formal test we can set for him. Such things should be our guide. If he can do these things with such skill, why should mathematics or reading be insoluble riddles beyond his comprehension?

What happens to us if we believe in a child's fundamental

incapacity to learn? What happens is that we do not keep on trying to help him and he is forced to continue to seek ways to outwit us. We give up trying to gather our powers together to invent better ways to present our case. We lose by default and then blame our failure on the child. We are beaten before we start if we give up persisting toward our goal. The child gets what he wants from us!

The trouble with us lies in the fact that we do not differentiate intelligence from interest. Intelligence is only a *means* of getting to an end desired. It is the ability to find ways and devise strategies to accomplish what pleases us. It is our interest that sets our tasks for us. Without interest, we set no goal. It is a matter of common knowledge that so-called backward children usually know baseball averages with uncanny accuracy, even though their history teacher assures us they cannot remember past events! These children remember the plots of murder mysteries but cannot remember where they put their books. They remember promises we made to them years ago but cannot remember that they promised faithfully to empty the garbage as soon as the television program ended.

We, too, play dumb when we wish to get out of something we do not want to do. How many of us claim that we cannot talk in public, solicit funds for charities, serve on committees, or do other things in which we have no interest or of which we are afraid? Our own common sense and experience should have told us that we cannot trust what is said about mental retardation. Let us, then, be less eager to impugn the intelligence of the failing child, and more interested in our own failure to find effective ways to interest him in striving for the proper, socially useful goals that he should be seeking. If there is retardation, it is much more likely to be our own than the child's.

16

ONCE BURNED IS TWICE SHY

Yes, we have too few schools, classrooms are overcrowded, and teachers are underpaid. We must find solutions for these problems. But our worst problem is the persistent and mounting incidence of school failures. We must not allow children to go on failing in our schools, year after year. Daily failures grind a deep pessimism into the soul of a child. Why should he look with joy on entering a building where he is supposed to sit for five or more hours and face one defeat after another? Who goes eagerly to a place, again and again, if he knows he will be belittled and berated there?

What adult strives to be a part of a group where he always feels less than those around him, or continues those things he does poorly? Why should we expect a child to keep on striving in the face of failure? Watch any child who is trying to do something he has decided he cannot do because other children have been held up as doing it better. Observe his self-conscious, hesitant, apologetic manner. You will note that he acts as if his brakes were set—as if he were more interested in avoiding defeat than in tackling the problem. A few defeats make anyone cautious in approaching a similar problem. A few years of failure have a truly serious effect since they lead to training in avoiding situations rather than trying to overcome them. This is logical, for once burned is twice shy!

Alan was burned more than once and became more than twice shy. He was burned first in his home. For in the home situation there were very definite factors that caused him to lose faith in himself as an individual. This faith might have been restored in the school if his teachers had had eyes with which to see. But they didn't. So he was burned again.

Alan was the second child in the family. He had a sister several years his senior. His mother and father were both perfectionists, interested only in the best possible performance. Needless to say, they overburdened their children with their expectations. They demanded no less than one hundred per cent performance. It never would have occurred to these parents to think in terms of measuring from zero up. Unfortunately, parents are not alone in this mistake. Teachers do the same thing.

The sister had quite a headstart in school and did well from the beginning. She was praised and held up as an example of attainment. The mother was a crackerjack in her housework. Swift and sure of herself, she was impatient and critical of the efforts of her son, who had a lower degree of activity. His slower motions irritated her past endurance. Sharp words and uncomplimentary remarks were frequently the lot of this second child. In apelike fashion, the sister took up the sport of showing her superiority over her brother. She was never told to mind her own business.

Any child must strive long to perfect coordination during the early years of life. A swift-working mother with only one child may have time to allow the child to work out such muscle problems. The same mother, with two children and more responsibility, may make the mistake of hurrying the second faster than he can go with assurance. Born in a family where standards of excellence were a compulsion, given a sister who aired herself at his expense and a mother always going no-where—but fast—we find much that might give Alan a poor opinion of his abilities. Such undermining of his self-confidence and self-esteem would surely have to show up at a later date. It did.

Alan went to school and for several years managed to keep up with the school program. Then he began to lag in arithmetic. Naturally, at the first sign of difficulty in this field, the evil he had been taught to fear (that is, slowness) came upon him. His teachers were not able to see that his fear was the real problem. No, they just went ahead and added insult to injury by criticizing his slowness and his mistakes. They didn't have the insight to tell him that a mistake is simply a friendly invitation to try again.

Frequent criticism in school compounded the evil and succeeded in making Alan more timid than he was already. This led to an additional loss of an already too low stock of courage. So he adopted an even more hesitant attitude and went haltingly, if at all, toward this problem. Finally he gave up with hardly a struggle to remedy this slight defect. He failed in mathematics, of course.

It was bad enough for his parents not to see that his was a case of lack of self-confidence. It was worse for his teachers to label it a lack of mathematical ability and to announce to his parents that he was "untalented." They recommended that he be tutored, thus concentrating the educational emphasis at the wrong point, to the further detriment of the child. The parents, whose pride had been given a crushing blow and who didn't hesitate to let their son see their great disappointment, engaged special tutors, with negligible results. Why not? How futile to heckle a child at his weakest spot, with never a thought of building up his self-reliance as an individual! Under such tutoring, there could be little in store for the victim but fresh humiliation and indignities.

Up to this point Alan had done well enough in other subjects. Surely a child who could read with comprehension, spell, and otherwise manage to keep abreast of the class could not be considered feeble-minded. But because of their own irritations and frustrations, both his parents and his teachers, as well as his tutors, began to treat him as such—as if he were somehow organically retarded. They never saw the apparent contradiction. They were oblivious of the obvious and proceeded to transmit their pessimism to him. Being criticized and depreciated at every turn, he became increasingly discouraged and finally gave up training himself. He began to be unsure in all other ways, too. As a result, the rest of his schoolwork rapidly became worse.

He was suffered to continue school, in the face of one defeat after another, until he reached the eighth grade. By this time he was many years older than the other children in his class. The difference in age and performance was so great and so uncomplimentary to him that further torture could not be inflicted upon him. The only thing that came out of the school experience for him was that his understanding of life was now completely distorted.

Afterwards, feeling utterly inadequate, Alan came to depend more and more upon his parents and other adults, thus prolonging his infantilism and avoiding the responsibilities of maturity. By the age of twenty-one, he would not leave his home without being accompanied by his parents. If the parents refused to take him where he wanted to go, he retired to his room, threatening suicide.

Alan's father died, and this left him free to be even more dependent on his widowed mother. He went wherever she went and had no associates or interests apart from hers. This continued for a number of years until she remarried. Then Alan began to show signs of jealousy, as might be expected when a stranger stepped between him and his leaning post. Unpleasantness developed swiftly. To preserve the new marriage, Alan, when he was approaching thirty years of age, had to be sent to a home for feeble-minded adults. His extreme dependency presented a picture of feeble-mindedness, and it was so diagnosed. Unfortunately for him, he was not feeble-minded in the real sense, for truly feeble-minded children do not feel jealousy. To be jealous, one must be able to make comparisons. Anyone who can make comparisons cannot be classed as feeble-minded.

It is most unfortunate that Alan's parents did not have the insight to prepare him for life. It is even more unfortunate that our schools are not prepared to correct such mistakes when children are starting their first independent experience outside the home. In Alan's case, the most the school could do was to recommend tutoring, which became, in this instance at least, an evil thing. No one saw the coherence of things as they were developing. Under the existing circumstances, the most that could be done was finally to dump Alan in the catchall classification of feeble-mindedness.

When a child begins to fail in school, it is far more than the academic failure we have regarded it as being in the past. It is a portent of psychological failure and indicates that a child is losing faith in his own abilities. Discouragement stands astride his path, and he begins to avoid normal tasks and useful achievements while he searches constantly for loopholes or other means of avoidance. What could have been done to help Alan and to encourage him, instead of pounding him on the head with tutoring? He was eager to learn to ride a horse. This was a lively interest and would have increased his confidence in himself. He was adequate in some school subjects, but his ability in them was not used to give him confidence in his capacity to learn. Suppose he had never learned to do arithmetic? Because no one knew how to increase his confidence in this field, why use this failure to make him forget his general abilities with regard to other things in life? Nothing succeeds like success! Why could Alan not have been made strong and able as a human being? Why didn't someone help him to find self-reliance and competence in the areas where he was not too discouraged? He was excellent at fixing and repairing things around the home. Why take a schoolmarm's word for his "lack of intelligence" when he had common sense enough in other areas? Why not build up his self-sufficiency in other areas and appreciate his contributions in these fields? Why let him believe that if he could not do arithmetic he was worthless and could have no value in our community life?

As things developed, Alan's slowness in one area loomed so large in the minds of everyone that all his abilities were blotted out and forgotten. Humiliation finally stopped all his efforts. Now—fortunately for his own protection against us—he is smart enough never to try anything again!

This case should teach us not to use our own pessimism and lack of knowledge to dim the hope of any school child. Let us remember that encouragement will not encourage, nor praise or blame avail, until they are fitted into the scheme of things as seen through the eyes of the child. Let us understand that futility is compounded and discouragement deepened if we think of a child in a vacuum, as a one-ness thing, rather than a two-or-moreness thing. We shall not make the mistake, then, of destroying the child's usefulness in all ways just because we fail to find the proper way to interest him in arithmetic!

17

IT'S THEIR BIRTHRIGHT

As adults, our job is to concern ourselves with all the relationships a child makes and with all the ways in which he approaches the tasks of life—not just his approach to a particular school subject. When a child is failing in school, we will also find many indications of failure in other areas of his life. We can detect any mistaken assumption he has made about life by the things he does that put him crossways to useful activity. We can also detect the same thing from his omissions—that is, from the things he must do that he fails to do. All of his behavior will point like a weathervane to the mistaken attitude from which it stems. As long as he holds a mistaken assumption, he will behave according to it. It is our job to recognize and try to change this underlying attitude. We must improve his whole outlook on life. Then he will be able to relate himself constructively to those around him. If we do not do this for him, we rob him of his birthright.

The problems that confront any human being are not only personal but are also social problems, in a social setting. If an individual falls down on his job, it disrupts the activity of those around him, just as breaking one thread in a stocking results in a long run. There is no way to know where it will end. It is for this reason that no child should be allowed to leave school a failure, for we do not know either where he himself will end or how many other lives will be affected by his failure.

If the child has got off on the wrong foot at home, the school should be in a position to make up for the mistake. It may be the last chance anyone will have to redirect the child before he goes out into the world to make his way. As things stand today, some school systems have guidance personnel who are trying to put on blowout patches as the more serious cases come to light. However, the numbers of such personnel are far too few to be efficient, and the majority of schools have none at all. We must not depend on this approach. For when a child is allowed to leave school without a proper training and feeling for society, there is no way to reckon the trouble he may give us later. Failure in school as well as at home opens the door to neurosis or criminality in later life.

It is unfortunate for all of us that our schools are far from prepared to detect and alter, before it is too late, any mistaken attitudes the child may have toward life. On the contrary, the school may augment his difficulties and set him more firmly against becoming self-sufficient. The child who is still too dependent on his mother by the time he is sent to school begins to fight the school at once. He may regard the school as an overgrown bully who is trying to snatch his crutches from him before he can stand alone. Unless this attitude is altered, his whole progress through school is threatened, for he will not be inclined to lend himself to the efforts of his teacher. He will reject from the start all the demands she makes on him. He will fall far behind the class, and this will then become an additional reason for him to try to run away.

Teachers do the best they can under the imposing list of handicaps placed upon them. But they are only human, like the rest of us, and they cannot do the job alone. All adults should do their share in the preparation of a child for life. All

of us must somehow make the school a more adequate place
for the critical job it has to do. As things are, teachers are reminded, all too often, of their inability to achieve a productive goal. This was poignantly expressed by Naomi John
White in her short reverie called "I Taught Them All." * It
reads in part:

"I have taught in high school for ten years. During that
time I have given assignments, among others, to a murderer, a pugilist, a thief and an imbecile. The murderer was
a quiet little boy who sat on the front seat and regarded me
with pale blue eyes; the pugilist lounged by the window and
let loose at intervals in a raucous laugh that startled even
the geraniums; the thief was a gay-hearted Lothario with a
song on his lips, and the imbecile, a soft-eyed little animal
seeking the shadows.

"The murderer awaits death in the state penitentiary; the
pugilist lost an eye in a brawl in Hong Kong; the thief by
standing on tip-toe can see the window of my room from
the county-jail, and the once gentle-eyed little moron beats
his head against a padded wall in the state asylum.

"All these pupils once sat in my room, sat and looked at
me gravely across worn brown desks. I must have been
a *great help* to those pupils—I taught them the rhyming
scheme of the Elizabethan sonnet and how to diagram a
complex sentence. . . ."

It is terrifying to a teacher, as it is to a parent, to realize
that the child before him may possibly develop along such
paths! No child was born for such a fate. Those who arrive at
such self-destruction could have been saved if we had not
failed them somehow. We are all involved in some way in
such tragedies—if only because we have to pay taxes for law

* From *Clearing House*, November 1937.

enforcement, jails, mental hospitals, and the like. Children's failure to become productive touches every one of us. We cannot shrug it off onto the teachers, under the present school set-up.

Parents must do all they can to help the schools with their job. The least a parent can do is to prepare his own child in the minimum essentials of self-sufficiency appropriate for his age, before sending him to school. In numberless cases, however, parents believe the teacher should also be a baby-sitter for them. The more immature and unprepared their child is when he is sent to school, the more they expect the teacher to devote herself to him. The mother who has made her child dependent on her is often the one who screams the loudest at the teacher for the child's failures in the classroom. Teachers resent being degraded by such parents to the role of baby-sitters. An infantile child, bent on getting the special attention to which he is accustomed in his home, makes ten times the amount of work for a teacher. Often his whole energy is devoted to disrupting the class activities to force the teacher to give him her attention. The further behind such a child falls, the more likely his mother will be to bring pressure on the teacher to carry him in her arms!

Teachers would be lucky if they had only an occasional child of this type. However, the trend toward laissez-faire in the child-centered home has increased the number. Since these children are not prepared to be helpful in school and pay no attention to the teacher, they have the entire day to get into mischief. The result is that the teacher segregates the small band of more mature children who are interested in doing some work and who are prepared to concentrate on learning the subject matter. These she teaches in whatever spare moments she is able to snatch between quelling riots, finding lost articles, and other police duties necessary to keep the infantile members of the class from getting completely out of hand. By the time her patrol duties are discharged, the teacher has little time to teach anybody anything.

The parents of these infantile children are usually the most bitter about the teacher's failure to teach their children. If the teacher tries to discipline them, the parents are apt to become especially enraged. On these grounds alone, one wonders why any teacher continues on the job, considering the small pay voted her for this work.

Parents should give a child the understanding that he has no right to be a behavior problem to the teacher. No one child has a right to a larger portion of the teacher's time than another child. Parents should not accept excuses from their children if they have made disturbances in school. A mother of four children had the right idea in this respect. The first day of school, each year, she lined up her brood. As they were about to go out the door, she issued this ultimatum: "Go straight to school. Do what the teacher asks of you. You are not the only children in the class. She has no time for monkey-business on your part. If I ever hear that you have made any unnecessary trouble for your teachers, I promise I shall make twice as much trouble for you when you come home." She always kept that promise to them, too!

Teachers expect difficulties in teaching certain skills to children, but this is legitimate work and they do not resent it. They do resent the gratuitous troubles that arise continuously from the infantile children in their classes. They resent the lack of support and the tongue-lashings given them by some of the parents of these children. It is up to the parents not only to keep control of the children in the home but also to support the teacher in carrying on such control in school.

Of course, there are always some teachers who are so incompetent and sadistic that a whole class suffers. In such cases support should not be given. The parents as a body should correct any such injustice by demanding removal of this type of teacher. But normally, children who do their share behavior-wise in the class seldom attract animosity from teachers.

There is a special reason for parents to give support to teachers. If the teacher and the parent get into conflict over the infantile behavior of a child, the child will use the situation as an excuse to play the parent against the teacher, to his own eventual disadvantage. Parents could make our present schools twice as effective overnight without increasing the cost to anyone. All they need to do is to hold their children responsible to them for school behavior. This would at once cut the teacher's work at least in half. She would then be free to do the job she is being paid for and wouldn't have to waste her time in baby-sitting or police action.

Parents could increase the effectiveness of the schools further if they would forbid their failing child the pleasure of television programs and other distractions until he has caught up with his class in all his work. Many children are several years behind in certain school subjects, in addition to those thousands of children who are failing outright. These children plan to stay that way—if we can judge by what they do. Most of them feel insulted to the core if they are expected to do any schoolwork on week ends, vacations, or holidays. They expect all these times off, although at school every day has been a vacation for them, while other children have been working. Their entertainment should be curtailed sharply until back debts have been paid. The reason for this is that they will immediately begin to pay more attention in school and will use their time there more effectively instead of wasting it as they have been doing. Evenings for them usually consist of three or more hours of television and a half hour of dozing over the assigned homework. It should be just the other way around—three hours of work and a half hour of television! If children are convinced that they will not have their fun until they pay the price (doing whatever is expected and necessary for them to do), then they speed up their mental processes. They will apply themselves properly only when the problem is inescapable and they cannot evade it.

The parent's responsibility to the schools does not end merely with preparing the child for independence and standing behind the teacher. Parents must help the schools to keep abreast of our changing times so that children will be given the background for modern life. The school today is often not very different in form from the old Elizabethan grammar school, which was set up for education in the classics. Since the reign of good Queen Bess times have changed more than the form of our schools has changed. Schools have certainly not kept up with progress. They should be preparing children for living in this modern world. They should not be content with cramming factual knowledge between the ears of unwilling victims.

Almost two thousand years ago Plato gave us a concept of what education ought to be. He described its essence quite simply in this way: "Nor should any trace of slavery be found in the studies of a free-born man. In the case of the mind—no study, pursued under compulsion, remains rooted in the memory. Pupils must be taught in a playful manner, without any air of constraint, and with the further objective of discerning more readily the natural bent of their respective characters."

Any resemblance between the type of education Plato was describing and our present system of forced-feeding-of-factual-information is purely coincidental! Nor should one mistake Plato's statement of objectives to mean some kind of school where children take only snap courses that require no thought, no time, and no effort. Quite the contrary! In a school of this description a child would be given the privilege of choosing work in line with his natural bent. No one would tolerate indifference, laziness, lack of concentration, sloppy work habits, disturbance by others, and all the other kinds of behavior that are pandemic in our present school system. Any child who did not choose to be productive in some area would be isolated early for treatment. He would be treated for his character disorder (his infantilism). He would not be regarded as a case of mental retardation, as is now the case. In short, parents should reconsider our whole plan of schooling and should insist that it be redesigned for modern life.

Parents should realize that teachers, when they go to teacher-training institutions, are taught to teach subject matter. This is quite different from being taught how to understand and teach children. In these institutions they learn chiefly methods of presenting and explaining reading, writing, arithmetic, spelling, social studies, and other academic subjects. This is called pedagogy. It is in reality just a system of holy rights and observances to govern the teacher's conduct in the classroom, especially when her supervisor is watching her teach a lesson!

Most parents, however, imagine that teachers are trained to be child-guidance experts who will know how to break down the child's resistance to learning, if he shows such an inclination. Most teachers are entirely innocent of any such guilty knowledge!

In training institutions the student teacher is usually trained to rigid conformity. That is, she is not informed that teaching is fluid art, but rather that there is a "right" way or a "wrong" way to teach a given subject. Of course, some teachers, with experience, discover for themselves that teaching should be fluid. Some are particularly gifted. However, student teacher graduates are not selected for teaching vacancies *primarily for their ability to handle children.* Usually they are chosen for their ability to handle intellectual abstractions and academic material. Thus we have some teachers today who ought to be doing something other than handling children. They neither understand nor like the young, but chose the profession for no better reason than that they themselves had good grades in school.

Parents should recruit teachers in their communities who lead vital, interesting lives as human beings. Teachers should be granted the right to be whole human beings. They have a right to make human errors, too. Most citizens in a community would not themselves put up with the social restrictions that are put on a teacher's individuality. In some communities teachers are expected to act as if they were members of a strict religious order and are forced thereby into a hypocritical existence with no chance for self-expression. In these communities they have to behave as sad-eyed saints. Since they can find little satisfaction in their work or after hours, it is not surprising if they turn out to be poor educators, worrying more whether a child splits an infinitive or can spell *"veni, vidi, vici"* than whether he will grow up to be a useful, contributing citizen.

The goal of our schools should be to turn out good fellow men. No child should be graduated unless this has been accomplished. It is no help to turn out well-trained academic parrots, even if a sure-fire method of doing so could be found. When a child leaves school, the outside world is little concerned with the number of A's he received. It is concerned with something vastly more important. If it could speak, it would say: "Little man, what now? Since your birth you have been fed and protected by society. No one owes you this free service any longer. What are you willing to give in return for what has been given to you and what you want from others?"

The child trained in self-sufficiency would have no difficulty answering such a challenging question, for he has been preparing for it all along. However, the leaning, dependent, infantile young adult would take to his heels. He is the type who flees into neurosis, insanity, crime, drug addiction, or becomes a vagrant nonproducer to escape standing on his own feet. Half of the hospital beds in America are filled with individuals labeled "emotionally ill" who broke down at this period of their lives because they were not prepared to stand alone.

It might be all right for our schools to continue to create more classes for "slow" children if the demands of the outside world would also slow down for them! But this will never be the case. We have no choice but to stimulate children to be more self-reliant so that they speed up their movements to meet the demands they will have to face when they leave school. To do less than this is to invite crime and disaster on a wider scale than has ever been imagined. This is exactly what seems to be happening. We are discovering, with the increase of juvenile delinquency, what it means to "sow a wind and reap a whirlwind"!

We would like to tell you how Wallace became a brand for the burning when he was sixteen. He had a brother, Roy, who was a year and a half younger. Their parents were well-to-do professional people. They bought a home in a community where there was much wealth and affluence. Like so many modern parents, they felt that to give all was the way to rear their sons, so they both worked and sacrificed for their children. They did not want their children to suffer any deprivations. Unfortunately, this led to pampering rather than to training their sons to be self-sufficient.

Roy was better-looking and more aggressive than Wallace. He competed with Wallace to be the favored one. He succeeded not only in winning the approval of his parents but also of his teachers. Unfortunately, the parents, as well as the teachers in the school, began to make comparisons that were not flattering to Wallace. He was consumed with jealousy, which stimulated him to attract attention by hook or crook and neglect his schoolwork. He began to fail in school. In due course the school labeled him a "slow child." They mistook his lack of training in self-reliance for lack of mental ability. Needless to say, it did not occur to them that the jealousy factor entered into the school picture at all. And so Wallace was put in a slow class. Each year less and less was expected of him along academic lines. In this manner the school pampered him as the home had done.

By the time Wallace became a freshman in high school he was on a real sit-down strike and the situation had become critical. His academic failures and his poor conduct were now a matter of public knowledge in the community. His mother and father, being proud, could stand no more humiliation. They decided to enroll Wallace in a select private school in another city. They managed to persuade the school to accept him as a sophomore. It did not take Wallace long to establish a bad reputation for himself in this private school. As a result, he was subjected to recriminations and punishments by the school authorities that year and the following year. His parents scolded and sputtered, reminding him of their financial sacrifice. By constant reminders that Roy was making them very proud, they continued to emphasize the problems that had defeated him in the first place!

Toward the end of the junior year Wallace began to see the handwriting on the wall, which read: "You are definitely not senior-class material for this school." This led him to retaliate against the school by the infraction of their most important rule. Thus he intentionally provoked disciplinary action that would force the school authorities to consider expelling him. Before they could notify his parents, he returned to his home. His parents were out, which is what he had hoped, for he wanted to retaliate against them, too. He took what money he could find and the car from the garage. Before the evening was over, he had picked up some other boys and girls whom he loaded into the car, and they took off for parts unknown.

Later that evening the school succeeded in reaching Wallace's parents to notify them of what had happened. The next morning they discovered the empty garage. They were able to put two and two together by asking some discreet questions in the neighborhood. In this way they learned that some other boys and girls had disappeared, too. No one knew where these children had gone until they returned home after their meager funds were exhausted. They had gone as far west as possible on what money they had to buy gasoline. They had been without food and sleep.

This episode shattered all the hopes the parents had had for Wallace. Their habitual reaction of irritation now broke into bitter resentment. They realized that their own measures to control this son were exhausted and they must seek outside help. But what? Wallace refused outright to return to the public high school in his town. The private school refused to take him back. The parents sought legal advice. It was suggested that Wallace be placed in a school for delinquents, but when the parents were informed that they would have to surrender control of their son for one year if they did this, they were reluctant to put such a legal blot on his record. Then they consulted the family doctor. He suggested a child-guidance program. A counselor was recommended.

The counselor and his wife were about to leave for Canada for the summer. After consultation with the parents, the counselor suggested that Wallace be allowed to accompany him and his wife for an indeterminate period. This was agreeable to Wallace. On the trip to Canada no eagerness was shown to push Wallace with any questions. On arrival, a rowboat and an outboard motor were put in his charge. After several days of "friendly indifference" on the part of the counselor, Wallace, of his own free will, began to talk about his past troubles. The story of his long jealous competition with his

brother emerged, and the steam went out of the whole matter. It was then possible to give Wallace some insight into his
problem, to encourage him to believe in his own intelligence
and turn his head in the direction of more mature behavior.
After this, Wallace decided entirely by himself that he would
return in the fall to his public high school and try again. He
was then ready to return to his parents for the remainder of
the summer.

His parents were notified, and they came for Wallace. Before they left Canada they were given guidance and were
helped to understand how and in what ways their mistakes
had led to Wallace's misdeeds. They were encouraged to have
trust in their boy's intelligence and were cautioned to cease all
comparisons and favoritism.

The following September Wallace entered senior class and
graduated without difficulty. The emotional tide of jealousy
that had swept him into delinquency was turned when he was
encouraged to have faith in himself and to turn his attention
to more useful and realistic behavior. His parents and teachers
failed only because they had not seen his problem in its true
light.

The home and the school, good or bad, are a training
ground and a staging area for the struggle that is to come later
in life. They should both have the same goal of presenting
reality problems in microcosm to the child during the time
that they are with him, to help him find constructive solutions for himself. Neither should be warmer or colder than
the outside world. It is no help to a child to cut down requirements below what life itself will demand of him for survival.
It is the birthright of every child to be taught to struggle independently before he is sent out into the world of reality.
The world is not geared to run on sympathy!

18

THERE ARE "LITTLE TERRORISTS" IN OUR MIDST

It is astonishing enough to watch a mere human being put huge elephants through their tricks in a circus. But it is even more amazing to observe the degree of subjugation and subservience to which parents can be reduced by a mere child! It is not at all uncommon these days for a parent to telephone a child-guidance counselor and ask for an appointment. Then she asks in a quavering voice, "What reason shall I give him for coming to you? He won't come if I tell him the real reason for the appointment. Shall I say you are an old friend of Uncle Harry's or one of his daddy's insurance clients?"

How can a mere child control and intimidate his parents to such an extent? The worst part is that the parents see nothing strange in the submissive, cowed attitude with which they approach such a child. Society would be in a pretty fix if a policeman had to get the permission of a robber to arrest him and take him to the judge! But why should parents be afraid to tell a child the truth when the time comes to stop him from disrupting and exploiting the family?

How does a child get this apparently magical power to terrorize parents or to limit their initiative where his behavior is concerned? If the child broke a leg, the same parent would not pretend he was being whisked off in an ambulance to meet an old friend of Uncle Harry's! Why cannot a parent be as direct with a child in areas where he is compromising the happiness and the welfare of the *whole* family instead of just his own bones? Do such children really have a power so magical that it forces parents to sneak behind his back to save themselves and him? Or do children control in this manner only because parents have defaulted in the proper exercise of their own authority and responsibility as parents?

Unfortunately, it is the parents, not the child, who are at fault. A child will not lay down his whip as long as parents supinely submit to all his demands and fail to look after their own welfare as they should. It is not a child's job to see that parents get along well in life. They should not leave decisions regarding the whole family's pleasure or welfare entirely up to such a child. In cases of this kind the parent must be the final authority.

We are reminded of an unruly, fighting girl of nine around whom the whole family turned as the earth turns on its axis. Frequently the parents longed to go out for dinner instead of eating at home each night. Their daughter always succeeded in destroying any such pleasure. She did this by refusing to remove her dungarees and put on a dress. Her mother would not be seen in public with her daughter wearing dungarees. As a result the parents and an older brother all remained at home because all three allowed this child's negativity to control them.

If we watch these little dictators or little terrorists in our midst, we see that what they do is similar to waging war. Most of their attention (psychic energy) is diverted from solving their daily problems and is turned toward maintaining or protecting their privileged position against attack. Their wits are devoted to repelling any efforts to make them less dependent. They resist attempts to get them to participate as members of a team. They drag their feet and seldom seem to move in the direction of cooperation with those around them. Often they do not do for themselves even those simple things they know how to do—they do not dress themselves, comb their own hair, bathe themselves, or eat without making a problem of it. Almost without exception, they have few, if any, real friends. The friends they have are all too frequently others like themselves, who are equally difficult to their own parents. They just do not function in a peaceable, helpful manner!

When such a child goes to school he is not prepared to co-operate with others. Since our schools are organized on a competitive basis, the child's tendency to oppose demands is made worse. This may lead to disaster. He may give up trying because he dares not compete, in which case he may be mistaken as a case of mental retardation, or he may over-stimulate himself to get ahead of other children scholastically. These negative, dependent, fighting children are not free to develop any real interest in their work and in their own personal development. In either case, they will not be interested in contributing to the welfare of the class. Their aim will be to get all they can for themselves, regardless of the cost to others.

When we foster the fighting, competitive attitude a child brings to school with him, why should we hope that he will ever learn to channel his energies toward more social goals? How can we expect this of him if he is distracted by the pressure of competition? It is outrageous and ridiculous to place the fault on the doorstep of some mysterious defect of intelligence in the child. Yet if intelligence test scores are low, this is the reason commonly given. If, on the other hand, the I.Q.s of these failing children are high, the "emotional block" is invoked as an alibi for our failure to get through to the child.

The term "emotional block" has been applied widely to children who, in spite of high I.Q.s, still do not do well or are otherwise difficult in school. But this is only a jingle-jangle phrase and tells us nothing about how to help the child. It does not spell out either the problem or the solution. If diagnosis is to be of help, it must have the treatment implicit in the description of the difficulty. We have to give up depending on such labels as "emotional block" if we hope to understand the difficulties these children are having. Labels do not get at the root of the problem. The root of the problem is the child's generalized attitude of noncooperation. But if you ask teachers about this noncooperation, they sigh and say, "It is only one more symptom." It is a symptom—but it is more than that. It is the most important indicator of all. It is exactly here that we must put pressure.

To appreciate fully the importance of this indicator, we must put our fingers in our ears and watch what happens in the situation. If we hope to understand either the child's failures or his successes, we must watch him in his total connectedness—how he relates to all the individuals and to all the problems throughout the whole day. If we do this, we see that these failing children move away from cooperation. Their movement is not in the direction of participating mutually or of being a help. On the contrary, they live in a burdensome way that demands our special help and consideration most of the time. They never seem to know what constructive thing to do, what we want of them or how to do it. They regard every life situation as an opportunity for interpersonal rivalry with those around them, or retire to nurse their hostilities. There is no doubt about it—when we watch, we see these children are at war with their community!

In any situation, home or school, competition means that one person has put himself at cross-purposes with another and, to that degree, has become the "enemy" of the common welfare. None of us, of course, is completely free of the competitive spirit, since it is rooted in the society of which we are a part. But in spite of the fact that it is a part of our cultural pattern, we must realize that all human progress, whether it has been individual or collective, has come as a result of cooperation for mutual benefit. When emphasis is put on competition-for-academic-perfection (100%) in our classrooms, with the clock ticking off the minutes assigned for attaining this goal, the whole day is pregnant with embryonic periods that give birth to competitive striving. Certainly they don't give birth to cooperation for mutual benefit, since in each of these clocked periods there can be only win, place, and show, as in a horse race. And what happens to all the others? They are the losers!

Let us consider what happens to losers in a foot race. Let us say that ten children are to run around a track ten times. It stands to reason that each one of them could do this if he could go at his own best pace. In short, all could succeed. But the objective in a foot race is to see which one can do it in the shortest period of time. That being the objective, nine participants are condemned to various degrees of failure. Instead of ten children each running ten laps around the track and all succeeding, we have only one success. Now, in any race we know that some will stop without even making the required number of laps. They fall out of the race when others get too far ahead because they see no reason to continue when they are convinced that they cannot win. Since that is their interpretation, we could not expect that they would do otherwise. Furthermore, some of those who get near the goal may try to trip one another so as to gain the advantage. But in the end only one wins, and humiliation is the lot of all the others who tried but failed.

Now let us consider those who deliberately fell out early in the race because they convinced themselves that they were never going to get to the goal post first. There will be no great fear of failure if there is not a correspondingly great desire for success. An individual fails when expectations of, or demands for, immediate success are too exaggerated and he loses the courage to pursue the goal. Since he feels that he cannot win, he grows angry and jealous of those who are swifter and more successful. He is tempted to hold them back and often deliberately does so.

The description of the foot race helps us to understand how it is that all the participants in a competition grow jealous of all the other competitors. In classrooms where the emphasis is put on a child's doing the best he can at his own rate of speed and in a self-reliant manner, this does not happen. But in classrooms where the prize is given only to the swift and where emphasis is put on winning, this is exactly what does happen. When children in such classrooms begin to feel left behind, a web of jealous competition is spun around them. The more jealous they become of the success of others, the more obsessed they are with the fear of failure and the more likely they are to drop out of the race. From this point on, the teacher suffers the penalties of their jealousy, since their eyes will be on those who are getting ahead instead of on the lessons she presents and the course they ought to run. The hope of avoiding defeat leads them to avoid doing *anything* in the particular area where they have fallen behind. It is as if a high, thick wall existed between them and the dangerous subject that seems to threaten them.

This crippling effect of competition must not be overlooked. We take competition so much for granted that we fail to understand it at all. A large number of people believe it is constructive to stimulate competition in schools, camps, societies, and other groups. It is true, of course, that we cannot have a game of baseball, for example, without two sides competing against each other. And even so, unless they are almost evenly matched, it is not fun for either side or for a spectator. But neither side would permit interpersonal competition *within the team!* Competition among members of the same team would be suicidal for the team. They would never be able even to finish a game.

The members of a classroom should function as a team. The classroom is no place for any kind of interpersonal competition. Competition is the opposite of cooperation. Competition involves struggling against someone to overcome him, whereas cooperation means that each is productive simultaneously, for mutual benefit. Everyone in a classroom benefits by cooperation. But competition diverts and destroys even the so-called winner by influencing him to depend and lean on his competitors. He loses his own self-reliance when he diverts his attention to "beating his opponents" instead of doing the best he can in the work he is supposed to accomplish for his own development and future welfare.

In order that we may better see the evil effects of competition on a winner in a classroom, let us consider the Straight-A-Girl. She had been getting A's in school for most of the year. Suddenly she developed insomnia and began to complain of the difficulties of her life. Her parents did not understand why she was making trouble for them. Investigation showed that she began her disturbances shortly after a new girl had moved into her class. This new girl was equally as able as our Straight-A heroine to answer the teacher's questions, and thus she became a threat. Our Straight-A-Girl was so fearful of losing her position at the head of the class that she could not sleep or find any happiness in life. Her tragedy lay in the fact that she was trained only to fight against an opponent but was not prepared to work for her own development in a self-reliant manner. This helps us to understand how competition can be the death of self-reliance, and conversely, why self-reliance will not grow in an atmosphere of exaggerated competition. Competition of this sort is the Stupid Child of Fear. Fear breeds greater fear.

We can see how competition tempts us to watch what goes on around us instead of learning to mind our own business. The competitive child is constantly watching his brothers and sisters at home to see that they do not get more attention than he does. When he goes to school, such a child is just as watchful to see that no one gets ahead of him in preference. As a rcsult, he does little or no useful work and falls behind. This only makes him more watchful of others who might shame him. Thus he goes round and round in a vicious circle. He becomes less and less self-reliant as he falls behind. Finally he gives up all hope. However, this does not mean he gives up the wistful desire to outshine others.

To make up for his humiliation, the child who falls behind begins to elaborate ways of forcing the environment to give him some special attention. To hide his defeat, he tries to show his power and authority in other ways. This drives him to sabotage, in the vain hope of holding back the other children. He may sabotage with spitballs, pen points, ink spots, pigtail pulling, giggling, whispering, jumping out of his seat, making faces, clowning, pinching, pushing, fighting, and with countless other distracting and disrupting tricks.

These disruptions and disturbances in the classroom may be poor substitutes for success in the outside world. But in the classroom they constitute a kind of psuedo distinction preferred by these failing children to no distinction at all! At least they aren't overlooked. And they cannot be wholly undervalued since others are forced to concern themselves with their delinquencies. It is in this fashion that teachers, whose emphasis is on one hundred percent or winning and on quick performance, suffer the consequences. But it is cold comfort to realize that the punishment fits the crime.

We must ask ourselves, though, how to undermine the will to sabotage that these failing children have, how to free them from their negativism, how to move them from their wartime to a peacetime economy. Certainly the answer isn't to work only on the lone symptom of the subject or subjects the child is failing. Instead, we must work to alter all their warlike attitudes simultaneously if we are going to prepare them properly for being the kind of citizens who live rightly with their fellow men. In other words, we must deal with the whole parcel of resistances these children have acquired—with our help!

What insight do we need? First of all, we must be aware that these children are unaware. We must bear in mind that they cannot see the forest for the trees. We must appreciate that they are lost and cannot find themselves. We must work out techniques for serving as their seeing-eye dogs and leading them out of their forest. In other words, we have to dedicate ourselves to the business of coaxing them away from their battle fronts and of getting them to demobilize.

What techniques should we adopt? First, we should be aware that no technique works in and of itself. None that we might devise will work at all, of course, until or unless we ourselves feel more friendly toward such children and become independent of them. We have to play the game of life more fairly with them by never underestimating their potential ability. We have to make our homes and our classrooms places where they are not humiliated and degraded. We must see that they find well-earned success experiences rather than a series of defeats. We must arrange to give them work in such a manner that all can do it and all can be winners!

To help us, it might be well to recall the story in Lewis Carroll's *Alice in Wonderland* called "A Caucus Race and a Long Tail," a part of which is about winners:

" 'What I was going to say,' said the Dodo in an offended tone, 'was that the best thing to get us dry would be a Caucus Race.'

" 'What *is* a Caucus Race?' said Alice; not that she much

wanted to know, but the Dodo had paused as if it thought that *somebody* ought to speak, and no one else seemed inclined to say anything.

" 'Why,' said the Dodo, 'the best way to explain it is to do it.'

"First it marked out a race-course, in a sort of circle, and then all the party were placed along the course, here and there. There was no 'One, two, three and away!' but they began running when they liked and left off when they liked, so that it was not easy to know when the race was over. However, when they had been running half an hour or so, and were quite dry again, the Dodo suddenly called out 'The race is over!' and they all crowded around it, panting and asking, 'But who has won?'

"This question the Dodo could not answer without a great deal of thought, and it stood for a long time with one finger pressed upon its forehead while the rest waited in silence. At last the Dodo said, '*Everybody* has won and *all* must have prizes.' "

Somehow we must organize home and school life like the Caucus Race, so that all our children are winners. How can we accomplish this? First, we must serve as a mirror so that our warlike children see their behavior for what it is. The mirror must reflect back to them the sad truth that the disruptive performances and the cheap heroics they offer in lieu of contributing something useful are no more than tooting on a penny whistle.

As things stand, the most appreciated child in the class is one who learns the fastest. Teachers and parents alike beam on him and frown on the ones who learn less and slower. If we are to maintain such a mistaken attitude, then we cannot hope to make every child a winner. We should aim in another direction. Our target should be self-reliance in accordance with age. Every child who wills to do it can find the way to be self-reliant. When we set this attainable goal for all alike and evaluate each child in relation to this achievement, then we will get peace and productivity because each can then afford to mind his own business and to grow up!

With such a target a child avoids asking for help when none is needed, and he avoids needless troublemaking because by such conduct he would express himself as infantile in the eyes of those around him. This gives him an incentive to struggle to improve himself and not give up easily in the face of difficulties. He can feel his own growing self-reliance, so that he is constantly encouraged from within to keep working toward greater competence. All his relationships improve, including his approach to his school subjects.

There are many ways by which we can show a child his infantile behavior, in contrast to behavior that would be self-reliant for his age. When we do this we must be matter-of-fact and give him permission to dislike us if he chooses. The child who has been getting away with murder—of one sort or another—is not apt to like the person who makes him toe the mark. If he tries to make us the villain, we must decline the role and point out to him that the job to be done is *his* boss as well as ours. We must help him to understand that although we are not his boss, neither are we going to be his servant.

If we ourselves keep clearly in mind that the target for our efforts is self-reliance for the child, we shall invent techniques as we play along with him. This is done mostly by two concomitant movements on our part: (1) we become as slippery as a greased pig when he wants to put us to work for him; and (2) we challenge him to try to stand up without holding onto us as if we were his crutch. In short, we escape from our enslavement to him by backing out gracefully from the tasks he tries to put on us, all the while pointing in the other direction, toward his need for developing self-sufficiency. In this way we help him escape from enslavement by jealousy and failure.

We shall reap rich rewards, instead of penalties, when we make this our goal. Once these children who have been failing begin to be productive, they begin to feel like individuals in their own right. They feel like property owners and are free of the competitive jealousies that held them when they felt impoverished. When they no longer have the need to concentrate on jealous competition and their consuming fear of failure, they have time, interest, and energy to learn. They will learn rapidly because they will enjoy the learning process in such a scheme of affairs. They will feel as if they had come into a fortune. Their temptation to sabotage those around them will no longer be the dominant factor in their lives, for they will no longer be in the position of debtors who have to fear each other—or us. When we thus enlist their energies under the banner of self-reliance, their goals become social goals. Then they are no longer terrorists out to ravage the rich fields of their neighbors.

19

THE "QUIET ONES" FIGHT US, TOO

Not all of our failing children are terrorists who openly assert their opposition to us. Some express their hostility in a more oblique manner. They are the Quiet Ones, who withdraw from the race and sit on the sidelines. Teachers often find the Quiet Ones the lesser of two evils because they don't make a rumpus in the classroom. They are frequently given a good deal of mistaken credit for being cooperative. Nothing could be farther from the truth, for although they behave less noisily than the Little Terrorists, their goal and direction is the same. They do not do their job, either, and must be carried as a liability in the group. Both these types of children are on a psychic detour. Neither is functioning along the main path of mutual participation.

One of the most important factors in the character of any individual is his degree of activity. The Little Terrorist has a high degree of activity. On the other hand, passivity is the hallmark of the Quiet Ones.

The outstanding character trait of the Quiet One is his passive resistance toward doing anything useful for himself or others. He plans to evade his tasks in life. The Mock Turtle described this pattern very well in *Alice in Wonderland*. He was discussing school with Alice and the Gryphon. The conversation went like this:

" 'And how many hours did you do lessons?' asked Alice.

" 'Ten hours the first day,' said the Mock Turtle, 'nine the next and so on.'

" 'What a curious plan!' exclaimed Alice.

" 'That's the reason they're called lessons,' the Gryphon remarked, 'because they LESSEN from day to day.'

"This was quite a new idea to Alice and she thought it over a little before she made her next remark. 'Then the eleventh day must have been a holiday.'

" 'Of course it was,' said the Mock Turtle.

" 'And how did you manage on the twelfth?' Alice went on eagerly.

" 'That's enough about lessons,' the Gryphon interrupted in a very decided tone."

Our Quiet Ones say the same thing to us on an action level, and just as decidedly. If they said it in words they would say just what the Gryphon said, "That's enough about lessons." For them, every day is an eleventh day, a lessonless day. We often find in this group many only children or pseudo-only children (those who have brothers or sisters five or more years older who appear to the child like parents rather than brothers and sisters). The only child frequently has a low degree of activity. Everything is furnished him, without effort, by his parents. Because of his position, he is often over-protected and overhelped. Consequently, before he tries at all, he waits for the help to which he has grown accustomed. When he goes to school or becomes a part of any group where he must share facilities with others, he faces competition for the first time. In such situations he expects the same amount of undivided attention from others that he has had from his parents (and any grown-up brothers or sisters there may be in the family). Since he has had no training in self-sufficiency, he is apt to respond, "I can't." And to himself he says, "And I won't try, either."

In the beginning this usually wins him special privileges and the teacher's special attention, at the expense of other children in the group. So his pattern of helplessness is rewarded and reinforced. He wins help in an illegitimate way rather than legitimately. But no teacher has time to remain his exclusive slave. Eventually he is referred to as "just a dreamer" or a "lazy child," given to daydreaming when he should be working. On his report card it says, "Unable to concentrate." What a canard! Actually he is overconcentrating —and very well—but on the wrong goal.

Too few people understand that laziness is an attack on others in the environment, to enlist their support. Laziness represents an excess of ambition coupled with inactivity toward achievement. A lazy person is not a person without desires, as commonly thought. His desires are so great that he feels powerless to achieve them by his own efforts. So he finds laziness the best means at hand for getting a half loaf from others, since he has given up his own initiative. The little he gets from others by saying, "I cannot," is more than he would get from himself for the little effort he is willing to exert. But he does not realize that his "I cannot" may eventually be regarded as the result of stupidity by those who do not understand that he is on strike against cooperation.

Whether he knows it or not, this is very likely to happen to him. For educational methods and thinking are still geared to the theory that the child who doesn't learn in school or doesn't try to learn, *cannot* learn. Parents and teachers alike, usually act as if such a child's brain is a small empty room with a locked door and an open window. They busy themselves simplifying and atomizing information and subject matter, stuffing them hastily through the keyhole of the closed-door mind. They hurry to fill this empty room, obviously against the will of the child, before everything blows out the window. However, in spite of their haste and best efforts, the information seems to blow out as fast as it is stuffed in. Then they really become panicky and resort to testing the child in an effort to find out what strange phenomenon is at work or what makes the draught that blows all their tidbits out the window. If the I.Q. happens to be high, "stupidity" can no longer be the label. Then it must be our tired old friend, the "emotional block," at work again.

The struggle continues. All kinds of nonsense are invented to exorcise this emotional-block demon, but it seems stronger than the charms used to rout it. The child goes right along doing nothing, as usual. Thus the child, the parent, and the teacher all end up exhausted on a heap of defeat. It was all useless, anyway, all those incantations to chase out "I cannot" when it was "I will not" all along!

When are we to learn that "cannot" may mean two different things? One truly cannot jump to the moon. Such leaps are not an inborn human potential. Nor could the capacity be acquired through training, unless our children sprout atom wings or some interstellar mechanism! However, the fact that a child does not read Sanskrit, for instance, only means that he *has not trained* himself to do so. It does not indicate that he has no inborn potential to do so if he chooses or *wills* to do so.

No one claims that failing children lack the intelligence to go to bed, eat, dress, bathe, and do similar things, even though sometimes they obviously will not do these things. Parents of such children are well aware of the sabotage this conduct creates in the household, in this respect. But why do these same parents and the teachers of these children maintain that it is only "stupidity" that prevents them from doing their schoolwork? It is time for us all to realize that the very unwillingness that blights the self-reliance of the child in eating and dressing has the same negative, contrary effect on his study in school. He will not do what is expected of him at home or at school. This is negative obedience and not mental incapacity.

His head doesn't have to be filled by us. He has done that for himself—with all the wrong things. His head has to be emptied because it is filled with resistance! We have to sweep out all the resistance cobwebs before we gain his inner consent to put anything useful into it. The Quiet Ones are discouraged children who will not take any chances. They have never been trained to be courageous and to stand alone. This doesn't mean that they are stupid. On the contrary, they are intelligent enough to avoid defeat and to get their own way at our expense—as who wouldn't!

Parents and teachers must learn to recognize "faked stupidity." It might best be described as situational. Now you see it and now you don't! It is a kind of sham death, such as we see in a snake called the puff adder. When the puff adder is attacked, it rolls over on its back and becomes perfectly limp. You would swear it is dead. You can pick it up and do anything with it, and it will not show a single sign of life. The only way you can get it to betray itself is to lay it down on its belly. Then it will instantly turn over on its back. It is convinced that it must be on its back to prove to us that it is dead. Children who sham stupidity betray their cleverness and their intelligence in much the same way. Their sham death and dead weight embrace their schoolwork, their chores around the house, and other things that we might expect of them. However, their cleverness and intelligence are apparent the moment they want anything of their own choosing. They mobilize ingenuity, memory, concentration, persistence, guile, or other energies to achieve their own ends or goals. And so, by brilliantly executed feints and sallies, they get what they want. We should be so smart ourselves!

Our Quiet Ones, just like our Little Terrorists, have given up effort on the useful side of life The jibes of parents and teachers, as well as contemporaries, have been aimed at them if and when they have tried and have failed in public. They have long memories of years of scoldings, humiliations, and social degradation that they have experienced by being compared unfavorably to more successful children. They have no hope of catching up. When hope evaporates, all of us give up. These children aren't any different from ourselves. But unfortunately, with their quiet inactivity they don't develop their potentialities. Instead, they sit and plan ways to hide their hurt feelings and anger under a mask of indifference or seeming stupidity. In effect, they prefer to be considered stupid than to risk any more public humiliation.

Our nagging will not help such children to become more active. Every stick has two ends, and no child can lag behind in every way if we stop doing things for him that he should be doing for himself. It is the supportive parent or teacher who must share the guilt for both his past and his continuing inactivity. One never sees a timid child without seeing a person standing over him with an umbrella of overprotection! The parent of a timid child must develop his own courage before he can help the child. He must develop the courage to allow the child to face fears alone, at times, instead of trying to remove all fears. Fears arise only when demands are made on us. A child cannot learn to face and to overcome fears if he is not allowed by his timid parent to deal with them. We can learn only by doing! Each person must learn to overcome fears for himself, because no one can do it for him. To shield children from reasonable demands (fears) does not help them.

Such children do not help themselves in any constructive ways, thanks to adults who do too much for them. And so it is we who should take the first step and learn to mend our mistaken ways—not the child! Until the child gets hungry enough to get his own glass of milk, we have to drop dead, as it were, instead of being so eager-beaverish to anticipate all his

needs, as we have been doing. Then these children will find
the profit taken out of their endless silence and inactivity and
give them up, of necessity.

Let us consider the story of Pathetic Paul, who was in a
private school that allowed him to do anything he pleased. He
did no classwork, and none was expected of him because he
was considered subnormal in intelligence. His I.Q. was 85
when taken in the first grade. When he reached third grade, a
second intelligence test gave him an I.Q. of 75. For this reason he was allowed to wander aimlessly in the halls all day,
with no one trying to teach him anything.

One day Paul indicated that he would like to ring the gong
that hung in the hall. When asked why he didn't inquire of
the school clerk in the office whether he might ring it, Paul
silently shook his head in discouragement. It was suggested
that she couldn't know he wanted to ring the gong, because
she wasn't a mind reader. But Paul insisted she could read
his mind. It was pointed out that this was nonsense, and anyway, how could he believe that she could read his mind and
know what he was thinking? His response was, "Because my
mother and my nurse can read my mind."

This was certainly a bewildering conversation. One might
be led to wonder if this boy was psychotic. The mother was
called to school. This conversation was repeated to her. She
furnished the explanation that cleared up the whole mystery.
"I can easily understand why he thinks so," she said. "When
Paul was an infant he was very ill. When he improved, he
was weak for a long time. We sat him on the floor and
propped him up with pillows. If a toy rolled out of his reach,
we retrieved it for him. When he finally got strong again, he
never asked for things he wanted. If we took him past a
candy store, he only pressed his face pathetically against the
window. We would then buy him something. We learned to

guess what he wanted, without asking him to express his wishes. We are still doing it at home."

The next day Paul was taken aside and some additional facts of life were explained to him. It was pointed out that his nurse and his mother knew how to read his mind but that they were the only two in the whole world who could perform such an amazing stunt. He was cautioned not to expect it of strangers, certainly, and not even of the school clerk whom he knew. He was advised to make known all his wishes in the future, and challenged to take courage in hand and ask the school clerk about ringing the gong the next time it was to be rung.

Paul did not, of course, demand to ring the bell the very next day, because he had no pattern of self-assertion. However, he did an unexpected thing. His pockets were always filled with bits of string, marbles, and the precious trivia boys collect. Though he had played with them endlessly, since he had nothing else to do, he had never offered to share or even show them to other boys. He must have had a hidden wish to do so, for that was the first thing he began to do. The boys, who had ignored him because he was so inert as a personality, now began to take notice of his presence. Now they had at least the exchange of trivia in common.

It was only a matter of a few weeks before Paul started to integrate himself into their social life as a friend. Instead of wandering all day in the halls, he remained in the classrooms with his new friends. Then he began to produce some schoolwork and to answer some questions.

Soon, to the amazement of his teachers, he became active and began to participate with his group in all activities. A year later, a routine check brought out an I.Q. of 125. This time it was the school that disbelieved! Another test was administered, with the same result. There was no doubt about it, Paul was an "intelligent" boy, one who had not realized it was necessary to communicate with others. He had thought life was a one-way street, just as it was at home.

Another Quiet One comes to mind. We will call her Lagging Lou. She was the younger of two girls in the family. Both girls were in constant friction. Lou had to travel to school with her sister, who wanted to take the 8:05 bus in the morning. Lou was always hanging back, which provoked her sister to a fury, since Lou's laziness often made them late. But apart from the constant quarreling, the parents were most distracted by Lou's refusal to answer questions. If they asked her to express a preference, she only shrugged her shoulders. They had to dig the information out of her. They thought there was something wrong with her but they were unable to solve the problem.

The answer was simple enough. She was being very successful in the light of her private goal. She was very jealous of her older sister and wanted all the attention for herself. And she was getting most of it by her tricks both at home and at school. The solution was to take the profit out of her silence. That was easy. Her sister was advised to take the 8:05 bus herself and not wait for Lou if she was not standing ready in the hall. Her parents were advised not to ask more than once about her preference in any matter. If she did not reply immediately, they were to make a choice for her and then go about their own business instead of standing around begging like paupers from royalty. The school was advised to do the same.

You may be sure that it did not take long for Lou to be prompt about everything. When she saw that the parade would not wait for her because of her delaying tactics, she was even ahead of time. Her tricks of sabotage disappeared. No one had to teach her anything; they had only to give her a reason for using what she already knew but would not use. When Lou's lagging and silence brought her disadvantages instead of profit, she picked up her bed and ran with it!

As they say in the mountains of Vermont, "My feet do not stand around while my body is being abused."

20

NEVER FEED A NEUROSIS

The children we've allowed to fail—those who openly defy the society of which they are a part or those who passively seek its shadows—are on a swift toboggan slide that may lead to lives that are frustrated and unhappy or may land them in our jails or mental institutions. If we would save them from this, we must first stop feeding their neuroses. The neuroses of adults start in childhood. A neurosis is a flight from social responsibility and productivity. It is a hidden attack on authority and a roadblock to cooperation.

Many of our child-centered homes of today are seedbeds for neurosis. This is not to say that all the children in such homes sprout a neurosis. Some find the path to self-reliance in spite of our mistakes. But the muddy background of such homes tends to be rich soil for growing Little Irresponsibles. When parents—who, after all, create the soil and climate in these homes—forget to protect their own rights as individuals from being usurped by their children, it is useless to hope that the children are going to guarantee their parents' rights for them. Children are not born with consideration! They will take from us as much as we will let them. If we default in the responsibility for patroling our own borders, they will move in on our territory and occupy it. This disputed no man's land between their needs and our own rights is fertile compost for the development of the "let George do it" attitude. If the roots of children are not deeply embedded in the soil of self-reliance, they are easily uprooted. And they wither quickly when situations become difficult.

For children with shallow roots, trouble begins early. School presents real work, to which they must give something of themselves. They cannot engross the teacher as they have engrossed their parents. The teacher cannot do their learning for them—nor can anyone, of course. School, to them, seems a harsh and dismal place in comparison with the moist comfort and solicitous service they have left at home. There are gardeners who have the reputation of having a "green thumb" for growing plants. But relatively few teachers in classrooms possess a green thumb. They certainly do not want a garden of little plants that twine around and cling to them. The teacher therefore often appears like a predatory beast to children so tenderly handled and so mistakenly reared in their homes. She bites when they try to exploit her! This leads them to resist her, in retaliation. It is not long before these children fall far behind because they prefer to bypass such a beast. They do not look at or listen to the lessons she presents. This is their revenge. They believe they are punishing the teacher if they do not do as she requires.

Teachers are only people, like the rest of us. Their training does not concentrate on teaching them human management —the type of "gardening" that is expected of them today. About the most they can do, when confronted by such Little Irresponsibles, is to fall back on their subject methodology. They search for some energizing lesson plan that may catch the interest of the child. Unfortunately, he is interested only in enticing the teacher into his own blind alley. Such efforts to interest the child rarely work, and so the teachers feel utterly at a loss to help. With a feeling of defeat, they put their not-so-green thumbs to their noses and glare gloomily at these children!

The mutual failure of child and teacher comes from the fact that they are not seeking the *same goals*. The goal of the teacher is to impart information that she knows the child will need in order to function independently. But the neurotic child's goal is to domesticate this threatening beast of a teacher. He wants to tame her to become a docile beast of burden like his parents. Each thinks the other is malicious or stupid and must be given as wide a berth as possible. Finally, the teacher notifies the parents that their child is failing and demands that they help this inept child of theirs with his schoolwork.

Whenever teachers make such an announcement and such a request, parents are thrown into a real tizzy. To be told that the children to whom they have given birth are below average is to threaten whatever pride such parents may have in themselves and in their children. Since parents have been so well coached by mistaken propaganda that they must give their children every special consideration and special attention, lest they feel rejected, these parents' customary response in such situations is one of subservience. They do what they think the teacher tells them to do!

When parents capitulate to this demand, the child successfully shoves the last vestige of his own responsibility back onto his parents. Since they have been in the habit of carrying him on their backs, he sees no reason why they shouldn't continue. So he ends up just about where he was when he was born. His parents didn't expect anything of him then, either! Unfortunately, neither the teacher nor the parents see the vicious circle in which they are now caught. Not only do the parents end up having more responsibility rather than less, as should be the case, but the teacher ends up correcting the parents' schoolwork. All fail to see the real problem as one of infantile irresponsibility and fail to realize that they are only fostering more of the same.

The day will come, perhaps, when schools will be prepared to catch up or repair mistaken development in those children whose parents have not trained them successfully for self-reliance before sending them to school. But that day is not yet. When a teacher notifies a parent that his child is lying down on the job at school and needs help, a parent should not start doing the child's schoolwork for him or trying to teach school at home. The parent, instead, should find a way to get the child to face up to his irresponsibility.

Help with schoolwork might be called the stage of secondary gains. If our house burns, it is a disaster and we are upset. But if we can build another house with the money we get from the insurance company or live rent-free with a neighbor, then these are secondary gains. This is essentially what happens to the child who doesn't do his schoolwork. The help his parents give him is the secondary gain he derives from his failure. He discovers the great value in remaining helpless. Failure and helplessness become a kind of vested interest to be safeguarded at all costs. The new arrangement between teacher and parents pays extravagant dividends for the simple investment of continuing to fail in school. Why should we be surprised when we find that the child shows no sincere will to improve?

Such a child draws these dividends only as long as he remains backward. An effort to work independently would expose him again to making mistakes and to adverse judgments. He knows a good thing when he has it. Nothing can persuade him to use his own initiative again as long as his neurosis is fed on such a lavish scale. He knows that his humiliated parents will fetch and carry for him. Why should he give up the established gains of the current situation for the unknown possibilities of fighting it out alone?

It is these secondary gains that lend reinforcement to the will-not. A child would be nothing short of a sucker to give up this illicit profit! And he isn't going to give it up until his parents and teachers deprive him of it. They have to make it more profitable for him to try than it is for him to refuse or to run away. For these secondary gains act as an anchor. If teachers and parents remove the anchor, the child is set free to sail on his own. All they have to do—which doesn't seem so much—is to say very matter-of-factly, and mean it, "From here on out, son, schoolwork is *your* job. You'd better see that it is done, because we are going to amputate your secondary gains right now!"

Parents forget that the failing child has more time to play, look at television, and loaf than the child who is discharging his rightful responsibilities. In most cases, children who fail in school also do less work around the house than the children in the family who study long hours and do their chores in addition. Just because a child will not do his school home-work, it surely does not mean he cannot dry dishes or do other equivalent nonacademic jobs. To amputate the secondary gains of such children, parents must see that they are kept at some kind of work for at least as many hours as they would be working if they did their real job of studying. This would give them incentive for doing what they should be doing at school instead of loafing both in school and at home. It disposes of the current ghastly situation in which they *do nothing either place!* When finally cornered and faced with the responsibility of being some kind of help instead of a complete burden—at whatever level they *can* be of help—they usually choose to be more attentive to schoolwork. They begin to think of the advantage of going ahead in school, and also begin to enjoy participating in the mutual responsibility of family work.

Wherever a failing child is found, we must look to the one

who stands closest to him and who supplies the subsidy. If he is less responsible than we can expect a child to be at his age, we may be sure the person on whom he leans has been shouldering this extra share of responsibility. Who else could be the guilty party? The child has no reason to grow further. Instead of pointing the finger of scorn at him, why not unmask the one who cripples him so shamelessly? The adult, at least, must learn better! Which of the two is the more seriously retarded or the one with the feeble mind?

This whole mistaken way of living together—the child, his parents, and the school—must be redesigned to cut out the child's illicit profits all along the line. His noncooperation must not be allowed to pay him dividends in ease or comfort. We must be prepared for strong resistance and sabotage in the beginning. For at first the child will seem to hate us, threaten us, swamp us with tears, and use every weapon at his command to intimidate us into becoming his servants again, as we were in the past. Nonetheless, the whole situation must be put on a cash-and-carry basis. He must learn the pay-as-you-go plan of life. Only the infantile individual expects something for nothing. The outside world does not run around picking up after us or rewarding us for nothing, as some misguided parents do. Again, we say that parents too often forget that they are supposed to be training children for the outside world.

Parents are apt to have a flattering picture of themselves. They imagine that because they are older, stronger, taller, and so on, they are superior to the child. This pleasant delusion is not supported by the facts of everyday experience with infantile children. In a child-centered home, it is the child who dictates and holds the balance of authority over the parents. He has the deciding vote as to what he will do or will not do, and uses it. He is the boss—not they!

Parents put on a very good and a very entertaining drama

for such children. The frustrated, exploited parents go around in circles—advising, explaining, reminding, urging, admonishing, cajoling, shrieking, scolding, and mostly begging on their knees—pleading for their Little Irresponsibles to do this or that. Instead of the child going about his own jobs in the home and at school, on his own initiative and under his own steam, the parents push or pull him, as a tugboat tows barges or an engine pulls boxcars up a hill. In any case, there is much puffing and panting by the parents. Some wit has said, "The road to success is crowded with parents pushing their children in front of them."

Moreover, parents hang on to a blind faith that if they repeat something just one more time it may work. It would be better to assume that the child has a convenient inner hearing-aid that he automatically turns off the very moment the parent opens his mouth. The child senses that his parents will not do anything more drastic than they have done in the past, even though they go on talking and threatening. His failure to change indicates that he has turned a deaf ear. His behavior says to them, "You talk too much!" And why should he listen? Children learn from what we do, not what we say. The silent parent who acts without talking is the one who is heard!

When parents have slipped to the bottom and the child is on top, the parents must get up off their knees and give up their begging position at the child's feet. The child cannot hold the top position if his parents stop paying him blackmail in order to stop his tears, fears, and tantrums. Nothing is gained by trying always to make it easier for the child. It is pathetic to see the extraordinary lengths to which some parents go to simplify problems for children. In return for such efforts the child only casts a bored, if not annoyed, glance in their direction and then says, "I can't" or "I forgot." On that basis, with no sincere effort of any kind on his part, he is excused from all responsibility, not only from what he *can* do but also from what he chooses to reject.

Many of these children, for example, blandly announce to their parents that they have no homework to do because the teacher made no assignment for that day. This may or may not be a fact. It doesn't, however, occur to the parents of failing children that since they are far behind the class, they should at least be studying the front of the book, which they do not know, in an effort to catch up to date. In such a case, why should any child or any parent wait for an assignment? The child is issued a license reading: No work tonight. That's exactly in keeping with his expectations. Television is more important. As he sits and watches television, there should be a sign posted: Genius at work. For he gets just what he wants.

If the teacher does give a class assignment, the situation is no better. The whole family has to use blasting powder to get the child out of his favorite chair by the television set. Then they must take turns digging into his books for him. He has usually forgotten what page the lesson is on and what is expected of him. Finally someone discovers the secret, and his body is put in front of the book and the book is opened to the right page. But his mind is in the other room, on the television program he is missing. His ear is stretched out the door into the living room, trying to catch a word or a gunshot now and then. By morning every wisp of information dug up and drilled into him by his parents has floated away. Only the parent bitterly remembers the lesson! And only the parent is worried about how the child will do in school that day.

Such a situation is much like that of the tenant who was far behind in his rent. Finally, his landlord rang his bell and said, "Mr. Jones, I am much worried about your long non-payment of your rent." The tenant looked at the landlord brightly and said with enthusiasm, "I am more than relieved to hear you say that. I, too, have been worried. Now then, there is no sense, is there, in both of us worrying? So I shall sleep easily tonight and from now on, and I'll let you do the worrying for me." So it is with these Little Irresponsibles who leave the worrying to their parents. Sweet revenge, theirs. Nice work if you can get it!

It is time to see that there is a vast difference between a child who has a problem and a child who *is* a problem. The child who is allowed to fail does not really have a problem— at least not yet. But he *is* a problem to everyone but himself. This has come about because grownups have been captured by his "I cannot." They have bowed to his wishes and demands. They have so served him that he is convinced he was ordained to be served. Even though they scold and storm at him, they go on serving his "cannot." He becomes even more angry and more resistant because he doesn't really understand why they're scolding and storming at him. They never taught him, by their actions, that schoolwork is his job. What they have done actually is capitulate and do his job for him, allowing him to escape serving himself, to have an easy situation, and to become a problem to them. This is why, later, he becomes a problem to himself.

We can see that the child who *is* a problem is like an animal who digs his hole with many exits so that he can escape in any one of many directions if we try to corner him. Our main job is to change the situation so that he becomes a child who *has* a problem—the problem of maintaining himself without our endless subsidy. We must close every escape hatch except the one into self-sufficiency. If we fail to do this early enough, we may be in the situation of the parents your authors know who have a son of twenty whom they continue to support in idleness. He sleeps most of the day until it is time to go to the races, where he gambles with their money. They are afraid to cut off his subsidy of food, clothing, shelter, and gambling money lest he become a criminal. We can only wonder what he will do when they die, and whether the kind of blackmail he holds over them is far short of criminality. All they are really doing is putting off the day when he will have to face the consequences of his unproductive activity. When they die he will finally *have* a problem instead of *being* a problem.

We cannot afford to waste any more time trying to overcome children's resistance to our educational efforts. This resistance has come into being through the unholy alliance between the child-dominated home and the I.Q.-dominated school. Both are inadequate to the job. Both must be rehabilitated so as to focus on the same goal of education. The primary function of both should be the same—to foster self-propelling children. Until now, both the home and the school have been putting emphasis on education from the ears up instead of educating children to live as good fellow men, to give as much as they take, and to live and let live. Unless children learn such a way of life, how important is it to teach them the parsing of sentences or the date of the Battle of Hastings? We must always remember that the child who passes the buck is an unhappy child, and if that condition is not changed he grows into an adult who tries to meet the demands of living by passing the buck and who is an unhappy adult. All too frequently children use between-the-ears knowledge to menace us. Our children are becoming clever and dangerous rascals!

21

IN THE LOOKING GLASS

We must devise a new way of measuring both adults and children. Until now, we have measured people chiefly by two yardsticks: those of chronological age and mental age. However, these two yardsticks are not enough to give us a clear picture of any individual. With only these two we cannot wholly understand many things about a person. We often hear someone ask, "How can a person of his education be such a fool?" We assume mistakenly that anyone with a college education will automatically know how to behave in a mature manner. Actually, to get the total picture of a person we must have a third yardstick: the measure of a person's self-reliance or self-adequacy. It could be called the acting-age or the behavior-age yardstick. The main thing is to understand that it is a measure of a person's independence or dependence. With this new way of looking at ourselves and others, we can quickly and easily see the whole situation.

There is an old saying, "Never send a boy to do a man's job." If we adopt our new yardstick, we shall stop sending a person to do a job with no preparation except a high I.Q. and a proper chronological age. If a child is nine years old and has a high I.Q. but must be watched and helped like a child of six or less, we shall not expect him to conduct himself as a fourth-grade pupil. In fourth grade he must have a greater degree of independence than he has been trained to assume.

He will either flounder or make trouble for us unless we manage to stimulate him to *act his age* in terms of self-help. It would be more appropriate and realistic to group children in our schools on the basis of their acting age than to group them on either chronological or mental age, as we now do. If we were to do this, it would give our children a better reason to behave properly. Of course, we would probably find that in self-reliant, healthy children all three ages would be pretty much the same.

But as it is now, schools busy themselves shuffling I.Q. scores as if they were a deck of Canasta cards, while many of the children in the classrooms are practically drooling in their bibs with rampant infantile behavior! Today too many school administrators spend their time in a statistical morass of intelligence and achievement ratings, report cards, charts, and graphs to prove that this particular child should be in a Rapid Advance Class or that particular child belongs either in an Opportunity Class or is CRMD material. (The letters CRMD stand for children who are supposed to belong in the Children Retarded Mentally Department.)

The so-called Rapid Advance Classes in our schools are far from being an unmixed blessing. A sharp blast of warning should be sounded for parents who consider entering their children in such classes. Only the most self-reliant and self-contained child can hope to come out of them unscathed, and our experience has indicated that there are not many such children in Rapid Advance Classes. The fact has been overlooked that not all children who get good grades in school, are *ipso facto* self-reliant. Actually, a great number of these children are amazingly infantile. And they are highly competitive, battling daily to get the very highest marks. Often their goal is only a feverish effort to beat other classmates rather than an attempt to learn. They feel that they have become the aristocracy of learning and therefore are haunted day and night lest they be put back into a regular grade. They are not aware that they are being ruled by their greed to get ahead or that the taproot from which their efforts stem is fear. When they get into college or on the job and fail to "fire the shot heard round the world," as they imagined in their Rapid Advance Classes they would do, damage may result. It may take the form of ulcers and other bodily manifestations, or they may go to pieces entirely. Ambitious parents take pride in such prodigies, about whom they can boast to their neighbors, but they should beware, as should we all, of children who have only words and no deeds as means of self-realization. Pseudo intellectualism turns no wheels and grinds no corn.

Most of the time, the so-called Opportunity Class is no opportunity at all, as it works out. It is set up for children who do poorly at some subject and for those who generally get low grades because they are nonreaders or reading problems. (Would you have any incentive to read if you were always allowed to have the seemingly more interesting diet of movies, comics, radio, television, baseball stadiums, and circuses?) In the Opportunity Class the diluted pablum now fed to children at the regular grade level is further diluted to homeopathic doses. The theory seems to be that if you cut down the dose sufficiently, it will seep in through the pores of the skin if given enough time and opportunity. But does it? Since less is expected of these children, they make just that much less effort. Here again, less, rather than more, attention is given to the development of the factor of independence. These children are treated more as babies than as the terrorists they really are! Children sent to such educational Siberias resent the infantile educational games they play, and they indicate this by their snail's pace of absorption. They know why they were sent there, and the fancy name does not make it more palatable for them. How can they achieve a feeling of human dignity or worth when they have no hope of being with their proper class? Did anyone ever stay happily in a Siberia?

CRMD classes are on an even lower rung of the educational ladder than Opportunity Classes. Here we find children such as Richard and Alan (see Chapters 15 and 16 in Part II). If little or no self-reliance is demanded in Opportunity Classes, even less is expected or requested of children in CRMD classes. The teacher functions as a baby-sitter and spoon-feeds them all day long. Such handling is not designed to stimulate or inculcate either temporary or permanent self-reliance. This factor is so far from being challenged that the teacher is only too happy if she can keep the children's noses clean. She herself has no deep conviction that she or anyone else can teach them anything. At any rate, such classes only mark a child for life. The pessimism of his educators is communicated to him. He comes to agree with them and dooms himself to irreparable self-doubt and feelings of shame.

Let us picture the change that must be made in our approach to the problem if we want to make any headway against our rising tide of failing and delinquent children. The teacher and the home must work together as a team with the main objective of turning out self-reliant, productive children instead of blaming each other for the failures. The teacher, in cooperation with the parent, will prepare a profile (see Questionnaire in Chapter 23, Part III) of each child. This will reflect his day-by-day behavior in a coherent picture or continuum that includes both home and school. We can see at a glance from this profile just how far the child has gone toward the goal of self-reliance.

We can see immediately any discrepancy that may exist between the child's chronological age and his acting age. It will show us all the areas in which we must improve our efforts to stimulate him to more self-sufficiency, to bring his acting age up to the level proper for his actual age. Short conferences between the parent and the teacher will inform both of them of the methods being used by the other. They can work together to plug up the many escape hatches the child has prepared to escape from his responsibilities. There will be time enough to worry about his academic progress and pump up his academic tires, once the many slow leaks in his initiative have been patched up!

The child, too, should be shown this candid-camera profile of his behavior. Profiles that reflect infantile behavior have a most stimulating effect on children who are deficient in their acting age. The juvenile delinquent, for example, imagines he is expressing courage and strength of a mature kind when he spits in the eye of authority. A profile of his behavior would disclose—even to his inexperienced eye—his childish dependence and lack of any self-direction in his choice of behavior.

It should always be kept in mind that children who act habitually in infantile ways are not aware that they are doing so and do not know how important this infantilism factor is. A child of nine who is still talking or whining like a baby is sublimely unconscious of the fact. How could we expect him to be aware of it when both the home and the school have failed to evaluate its significance?

There are doubtless many ways to chart and dramatize for a child his mistaken and infantile orientation. The authors use one approach labeled the "Limping Figure" because one leg of the figure is shorter than the other. If one leg of a child were actually shorter than the other, he would limp when he walked. This figure shows infantile children that if, for example, they are nine years old but act like a five- or six-year-old, they limp behavior-wise. This gives a child a yardstick for measuring his own behavior and challenges him to strive in a direction of more maturity. It also acts as an astringent tonic, for it gives the right perspective not only to the child but also to his parents.

Many adults may underestimate a child's intelligence, but we have yet to find a child who didn't understand the Limping Figure. In the following illustration we deal with a very dependent, irresponsible, leaning girl* of nine. This is her "behavior profile."

LIMPING GIRL—NINE YEARS OLD

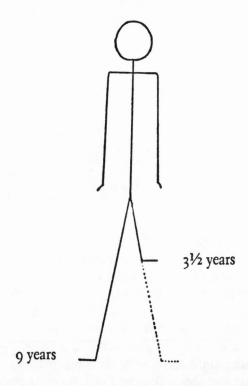

3½ years

9 years

ACTUAL-AGE LEG   ACTING-AGE LEG
                                  (Burdensome, baby ways)
                                  1. Talks like a baby (whiny
                                     voice)

* This is an actual profile of Helene, the "Bewitched Princess" in Chapter 22.

2. Hangs on and clings to mother
3. Carries doll or teddy bear everywhere, like baby sister
4. Has to be put to bed and won't go to sleep until read to
5. Uses nighttime and daytime to control parents and others
6. Has nightmares and yells to get into bed with parents
7. Dawdles about dressing and eating
8. Refuses to go to toilet alone
9. Never sits still; wiggles like a baby
10. Has temper tantrums, as if abused
11. Wants own way all the time; bosses all who come in sight
12. Doesn't get along with other children
13. Refuses to learn to read
14. Complains about schoolwork and insists on being helped with it

The acting-age leg is cut off and notched to the age of three or four or five, depending on what seems appropriate for the observed behavior of any particular child. It always bears the legend: "Burdensome, baby ways." Under this are listed all the ways in which the child actively or passively makes trouble for others. They must always be the exact ways in which he is a burden and does act like a baby. Such a list might include: must have help dressing, bathing, combing hair, tying tie and shoes; does not pick up own clothes; does not pay attention in school or do schoolwork, etc.; has temper tantrums; cries easily; sucks thumb; snaps fingernails; cracks knuckles; makes faces; screams at parents; clowns in school; is a poor sport; tattles; lies, cheats, steals; is tardy; wets the bed; makes trouble about eating; stammers, and so on.

Under the short leg there is a broken line that extends down to the length it should actually be, depending on the child's chronological age. IF and WHEN the child discontinues using any one of these tricks or learns to be a help instead of a burden in any one of these respects, the broken line is filled in solidly, bit by bit. In other words, when the child overcomes any baby way, the leg grows a notch. If a child chooses to behave as maturely as any self-reliant child his age, the short leg may grow until it is even with the actual-age leg. Then he can regard himself as being equal to any other child his age—and so can we!

The authors have used this figure with hundreds of failing children who needed a way of having their behavior mirrored for them, since they could not otherwise get a glimpse of themselves. As the figure was being drawn, before his eyes, we have always indicated and explained why the listings under the short leg were considered "baby" tricks and inadequate for a child of nine—or whatever age the child happened to be. But *before* that, we have always taken in inventory of any helpful, self-reliant things the child did habitually for himself or his parents. These were the evidence that he was not wholly infantile. We have stressed that these were helpful ways—these were his assets or "starting capital." A child is encouraged and challenged by such an inventory.

There is never a very imposing or long list of assets when one takes an inventory of the things a leaning, dependent, irresponsible child does on his very own. That is why he is a burden and a problem. It is not that he is unable to comb his hair! The question is, "Who asked him to do so or expected this of him?" This type of child moves in helpful ways only when prodded or challenged. To challenge him is the job of the adult!

When a child gains a coherent realization of his infantile limping, he is willing to work in the direction of "growing the short leg down." We have yet to find a child who has not felt this as a challenge and who has not been happy and excited when he resolved his problems and both legs of the Limping Figure came into balance.

We have used this figure with various groups of children in classrooms. In such cases the group itself made a list of the grown-up things they thought any child in their age group should be able to do. Then they listed tricks they considered "babyish" for that age. Thus the group created its own yardstick for measuring its behavior, and became its own disciplinarian.

Parents could benefit if they were to chart, in this way or in some manner of their own devising, the persisting infantilisms to which a child of theirs is still clinging. The parent should list at least the things that have to be done for the child, the areas in which a child his age should be functioning without supervision, the ways in which he disturbs the household needlessly, and similar claims for attention or support. When the list is complete it can serve as a map of the territory that remains to be covered in preparing the child for the outside world and its demands.

Whatever technique is used, it should be thought of as showing a child his own infantile behavior *in a mirror*. Once a child is given insight of this kind, he cannot engage again in such useless activity with a wholly clear conscience. For now he stands condemned in his own eyes. To earn his own self-respect, he may begin to hang up his hat and do similar grown-up things, even without pressure, since his erstwhile secret is now exposed to daylight.

This procedure has to be carried out through friendly explanation. It would only offend a child if it were used as a kind of nagging, or with humiliating sarcasm, or in any domineering, autocratic way. The whole approach must be as quiet as the mirror in our bathroom that tells us how we look. Our mirror does not find fault with us. But by showing us the truth, we find fault with ourselves! Then we are in a position to correct what it has reflected.

How fast a child's "short leg" will grow depends mostly on our cooperation with him. We must not forget that all life is a matter of training. If we have always served as a child's crutches, we must expect that he will bring up his heaviest artillery against us when we try to back out of being his support. But we must persist and must demonstrate that we are willing to be his friend, not his servant as in the past. We must insist that we have as much right to life, freedom, and the pursuit of happiness as he has. It will not be enough to say this with our mouths and then go right on picking up after him! He will judge our words by our deeds and will see whether we are honest in what we say. If he can throw a tantrum and get his way, he will disregard our fine and noble words, for we will have to show him by our actions that we are still willing to serve as his flunkey.

We should not expect that a child will wash his neck, for instance, merely because we no longer do it for him. We must bring some social pressure to bear to encourage habits of cleanliness. Later in life the government will use some such means to ensure that he pays his income tax. He may just as well learn now. If he insists that he likes a dirty neck, then we can make him twice glad by smearing some burnt cork or other dirt on it to help the game along. Let him wear this to school for several days. Even though he has had the final word at home for as long as he can remember, he will meet with limitations when he steps outside the house. Out there, there is less profit in being obdurate.

When a child finds that he cannot have his entertainment until he has discharged reasonable demands made on him, he will eventually agree that it is easier *to pay for his pleasures than to be bored without them*. Under no circumstances should we ever bribe a child to do those things that the outside world will demand of him *as a matter of course* in his daily life. We must not let him imagine he is doing us a favor when his neck is clean, his hair combed, his teeth brushed, and things of that kind. These minimum essentials are his admission ticket to being allowed to participate at all outside the home.

Few children have the will to improve as long as they can hang on to their secondary gains. Secondary gains are like income inherited from a rich uncle. How many people would ever have gone to work if they could have lived in comfort on unearned, inherited money? How can we expect that children will surrender their advantages as long as we supply them gratis with the fruits of our labors?

The one most important factor for parents and educators to understand is that "failures" do not exist in a vacuum. Someone stands by and supplies the subsidy on which they live. We do not find failure in the animal world because to fail would be to die. A wild animal must strengthen itself, overcome its weaknesses, and find its own way to survive, because nature does not subsidize persisting failure. Only the human adult has the habit of giving endless subsidy when a failing person refuses to help himself. We cannot help a failing individual until we begin to cut down on, and cut out, our mistaken subsidies to him when we find he is not using them to increase his effectiveness. In short, when a child is failing to develop properly over a substantial period of time, we may be sure that we are dealing with a case of SUBSIDIZED FAILURE. We must blame ourselves, not him, for his persisting weakness. Until and unless we are willing to undertake an amputation of his subsidies, we are in the position of contributing to his delinquency.

To be sure, no amputation is accomplished without some pain and risk both to the patient and to the surgeon. But we cannot allow our mistaken sympathies to stand in the way of our common sense. If an operation is needed to save a life, we must operate and bear the anguish as best we can. In most cases the amputation of failing children must be done by the parent to whom the child is attached more closely than a shadow! The parent and the child must become two independent producers instead of a producer and a parasitic growth that saps the strength of the producer. Each must find his own roots instead of one being rooted in the other. Let us describe such surgery with reference to the Limping Figure to show how it would go.

The parent must function much as a plastic surgeon does. If a plastic surgeon is to operate on a disfigured face, he must decide before he operates how the face should look once the operation is accomplished. So it is with a parent who has a leaning, dependent child. The parent must decide in what ways the child is being subsidized and what the child should be doing beyond what he is doing. Then, as the surgeon, the parent has to cut off the mistaken services being rendered the child. After the amputation, the relationship between parent and child should eventually become one of mutual sharing of advantages and disadvantages in the daily situation.

As we pointed out when we described the Limping Figure, there is always an imposing list of infantile traits that should disappear. In the figure we presented, we might say that the Princess went only ten percent of the way toward mutual sharing or a fifty-fifty deal with her parents (fair play, in other words). The parents were left to go ninety percent of the way, or forty percent beyond the halfway mark. We might diagram the movement like this:

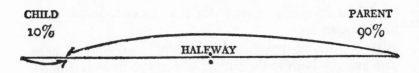

CHILD   **PARENT**
10%   HALFWAY   90%

Let us list: (1) the manifestations of infantile behavior; (2) the child's secondary gains; and (3) what the parent ought to do to amputate them.

INFANTILE BEHAVIOR (What Child Does)	SECONDARY GAIN (What Parent Does)	AMPUTATION (What Parent Could Do)
Talks like baby	Must listen harder	Ignore baby talk
Clings to parent	Drags child along	Refuse to drag along
Clings to doll	Tries to divert child	Take away doll
Demands to be read to	Entertains without pay	Stop bedtime reading
Calls from bed	Gives up free time	Refuse to answer
Dawdles dressing	Nags or helps	Put back to bed for day
Wiggles	Pleads to stop	Urge faster wiggling!
Has temper tantrums.	Placates	Urge to yell two hours!
Bosses	Obeys and submits	Mind own business
Fails in school	Tries to teach	Refuse home help

The suggested things that the parent could do are, of course, not the only ways to get out of the clutches of a grasping child. They are suggested to show that the parent must be like the greased pig at a farmer's picnic. The parent must become so slippery that the child can no longer catch him.

In other words, parents who have been in the role of captives must no longer plead with their jailors to let them out of jail. On the contrary, they must tunnel under their prison walls to find their own escape. In general, we might say that a parent ought to do the opposite of what he has been doing, in order to amputate the gains he has been supplying to the child.

To return to the Limping Figure of our Princess—the amputation had to be done in two stages because she had so many infantile tricks in addition to her school failures. The first stage was to make the Princess more self-reliant at home. Her parents refused to answer when addressed in a whining voice. They pretended they didn't hear, so the child had to speak properly to get a response. Since the doll and teddy bear were used by the Princess to divert attention or avoid necessary tasks, they both were put away, in spite of her objections. Bedtime reading was discontinued. Calls from the bedroom went unanswered. Dawdling was not rewarded by help, and the Princess was deprived of liberty for the day, since "babies" are not expected to have the privileges of self-reliant children. The parents refused to be unpaid servants any longer and announced that they chose rather to "be her friends."

As might be expected, the Princess sat and sulked when she was deprived of her crutches. She did not immediately give up her sabotage; children seldom do at the beginning of this process. Instead, she tried to increase her appearance of being helpless in order to tempt her parents back into servitude. For example, she would go off to school with uncombed hair and unwashed face, hoping to shame her mother into looking after her. It should be pointed out here to all parents who start amputating, that such a child's hair will look like a buzzard's nest for a while! Moreover, at this stage a child may begin to vomit, bite its nails, wet the bed, and do other things to terrify or entrap the operating parents. But these tricks of sabotage are of short duration if parents do not get the wind up or start running scared! If parents retreat, the child becomes an eternal saboteur.

Without an audience, the farce the Princess enacted soon became a bore to her—as it had been boring to her former captive audience. At this point she began to look after herself instead of expecting or demanding that her parents look after her. The freedom she gained allowed her an opportunity to join with her age-mates and make some new friends in the neighborhood and at school. She became quite happy, and discussed with relish the pleasure she found in these social relationships. She began, also, to show some improvement in her schoolwork. There was evidence that she wanted to be at the same grade level as her friends, whereas she was about forty percent effective. There remained the matter of doing homework. The parents were still caught in that trap. We might picture the situation at this stage as follows:

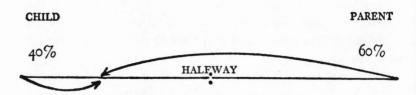

The second amputation is not difficult, once mutual respect and self-reliance have been established in the home. The parent's role now has to change from that of a private schoolteacher to that of *supervisor* of *finished* work. Adequate and proper time must be set aside for homework, and its regularity must not be interrupted. Radio, television, and similar distractions have to be ruled out. The child must go to his or her own workshop and concentrate, unaided, on the task at hand. Only when the task is finished does the parent examine it for neatness, accuracy, and completeness. Mistakes should be marked, but the parent should not enter into explanations. The child must be held responsible for asking the teacher the following day for the proper method or explanation. Only in this way is a failing child stimulated to start paying attention when the teacher is explaining things. Children of this type seldom, if ever, listen to the teacher if they know they can press a parent into an explaining service. Why should they listen? The parent must continue in the role of supervisor for as long as necessary—that is, until the child eventually finds out the proper way to do the homework chore. The job of supervising does not take more than a few minutes, whereas formerly it took endless hours that were spent in useless efforts to teach an unwilling and nonlistening child. As we can see, this step requires that the parent stop helping the child with schoolwork—or, worse yet, doing it *for* him, as so many parents today are doing! The parent must hold the child responsible for behaving properly in school, too. Though a child may not be up to grade level with his class, he should not be allowed to disrupt others in his grade. If he causes disturbances in school, then home privileges should be curtailed as a penalty until he learns to mind his school manners.

The child must be taught now to share some of the common tasks in the home so that he or she will understand how much thought and effort go into keeping the home running properly. This puts the whole family on a basis of helpfulness so that no one member makes work for another. It is in this way that the home ceases to be based on special help, special exemption, and special privilege. It is in this way that the home gets on a pay-as-you-go-no-credit footing. In other words, the home is:

A final warning must be added to what has been said. No ship can sail in a straight line across the ocean. If we were to

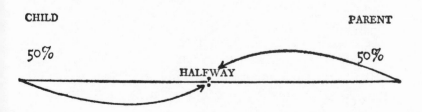

CHILD   PARENT

50%   50%

HALFWAY

watch it we would see that the line the ship makes is a kind of zigzag. At times it might seem to be off course. But if we saw the same ship from high enough up in the sky, it would then appear to be following a straight line. All this means is that in Operation Amputation we must keep the *direction* steady even though we may have to zigzag at times.

Operation Amputation might be compared in many ways to trout fishing. The trout line, hook, and leader are very light. A trout can break them easily if we tug too hard during the landing process. Only the most stupid fisherman would do this. The art of trout fishing lies in tiring out the fish by keeping a small, steady pressure on the line. When the trout first gets hooked he runs and jumps in fury, trying to throw the hook out of his mouth. If the line is slack, he will succeed. During the stage of his most violent fighting we must pay out the line as he runs in the other direction. But we must never let the line get slack. When the trout is less resistant, we must slowly reel him toward us until he makes a dash again. By repeating this process as often as necessary, the trout finally gets tired of fighting and can be landed.

Some squeamish adults like to believe that they can win a child over without any social pressure. It may be possible, but we have never seen it done with an adult or with a child. If a person has achieved a position of unbridled domination over those around him, he is not likely to be talked out of it by kind words. No painless way has yet been found to force a dead beat to pay his bills!

By the same token, it is neither harsh nor unfair for parents to use pressure on a child to make him uncomfortable if he defaults in tasks that may be expected of him as his share. The outside world will bring plenty of pressure on him in later life if he does not give in return for what he gets. It is better to prepare him for this early in his life so he will not be shocked or stunned by pressures when he meets them. He must not be allowed to believe that his likes or dislikes of necessary chores are the same as reasons. Parents should make it difficult for a child to default a debt without paying some price for failure.

These same squeamish adults usually confuse the issue by trying to equate the imposing of adult domination on a child with holding a child to its full responsibilities. These are quite different things. It is obviously unfair for an overneat, compulsive parent to demand of a child the same prejudices and degree of cleanliness he has chosen for himself. Nor does such a parent need to put up with filth that would make a Ubangi blush in public! As long as a child is not notably conspicuous at either extreme, he is probably doing well enough. Our final goal in the education of our children is to make them self-reliant and productive citizens in the outside world, and for this they do not have to become plaster saints!

Let us remember always that our children will soon be done with us and will go out of the home into the bigger world. If we truly love them, we shall want nothing more than that they do not hesitate, tremble, turn back, lose courage, seek evasions in crime, illness, drugs, alcohol, and similar things. Only if we have taught them to set their own tasks, work for themselves, and get along with their associates can we be sure we have given them some guarantee against being defeated easily. This is what self-reliance or independence means in operational terms. When they meet difficulties they will have the habit of self-starting and will find solutions for the problems. So let us not imagine that the most important lesson we can teach our children is to keep dresser drawers orderly or to brush their teeth three times a day. And may all the gods grant that we become as self-reliant as we expect them to be!

III

PERSISTING INFANTILISM
AS AN AFFLICTION

22

THEY WEREN'T BORN HOBBLED!

Relatively few children are born hobbled. Vast numbers, however, become that way after birth. We speak now of emotional cripples. We have said, and must repeat again, that when parents do not structure the relationships in their homes on a humanly straight basis, they cripple their children.

It is time now to present to you—as through a looking glass —four children who weren't born hobbled. The presentations will not be blow-by-blow descriptions of how to cure this type of children, but the treatment will be implicit in each child's history.

Each of these four cases will differ with respect to what the parents or teachers found to be the presenting problem (symptoms) that most concerned them in their dealings with these children. But though differing, the pattern of emotional crippling or persisting infantilism will be as apparent as a white thread woven into an otherwise dark-colored tapestry. It will also be apparent that the degree of infantilism found in each of these children is but a reflection of the degree of infantilism of their parents—at least in certain areas.

The first history is about a boy whom the truant officer was about to make a court case because of the boy's refusal to go to school. The second case is about a third-grader who was expelled from school because he was already a miniature thug!

The third is about a now-hopeless, though clever, boy who early in his life was considered by social agencies, his parents, and his teachers to be mentally retarded. The fourth is about a nine-year-old girl who ruled her parents and teachers by her abysmal failures in academic areas, although the school records indicated she was a gifted child.

The untrained, unaided eye might see only the dramatic and easily apparent differences in these cases. They may appear as four riddles devoid of any common denominator from which to approach them for solution. But with the proper lenses in our spectacles we can see the common likenesses. Here is the Rx. (prescription) for the lenses:

(1) Any child who is making unnecessary difficulties in his environment and who is considered by his parents and teachers to be a problem is a child who is suffering from the virus of persisting infantilism. This may appear in a multitude of disguises, such as desire to be the most loved or the most favored, lack of self-sufficiency, interpersonal rivalry, hoodlumism, vandalism, et cetera.

With these lenses you will see all four children as "clever rascals." Actually, they should be seen as greedy politicians or irresponsible gangsters who want to enrich themselves from public funds! They fight to maintain their apparent disabilities as if they were valuable plots of ground. Each wants to hold on to his miniature kingdom so that he may rule, get recognition, and levy taxes. By this process, it will also be found that the adults involved are tied down and impoverished, just as is the case under any unfair taxation policy in any community. In reality, the difference between a fair tax and an unfair tax is the *use made of the gains*. Taxes used to enrich everyone in a community are fair. However, taxes used

only to enrich some politician are recognized as unfairly burdensome, are fought, and are eventually eliminated.

Children who have overlong savored the fruits of dependency want to continue to enrich themselves in this manner.
Parents who want to rid themselves of such a child's unfair
taxation can do so only by having a Boston Tea Party of their
own!

THE CASE OF MILO—A BOY WITH "SCHOOL-BELL FEVER"!

Milo was seven, the older of two boys. He had the face of an
angel and the eyes of a wounded deer, but a breath of air
would have blown him away. His speech was that of an am-
bassador. He could follow the most complicated arguments of
reasoning and come up with a better-reasoned response. His
manners were those of a courtly gentleman of eighty. He was
charming company. But no power on earth seemed able to
move him to return to school.

At six he had entered first grade. He had liked school and
had done superior work. The following year he entered second
grade, somewhat reluctantly. One November afternoon, just
before the end of the school day, he ran out of the classroom.
No amount of pressure could get him to return. In May the
exhausted truant officer determined to make this a court case.
The parents were frantic. The father was fearful of losing his
job because he had already taken so much time off, taking his
son to behavior clinics. Now, when he had done everything
in his power, with no success, he was threatened with legal
action. No one could guess how this wisp of a child could harbor such ironclad determination. There seemed to be no reasonable explanation for his behavior.

Everyone who was or who became involved tried to think

of an explanation. They would ask the child, who would con
sider the question gravely. Then he would agree that it might
be the right answer but he could not be sure. Was it because
other boys in the class were bigger and bullied him? Well, perhaps. On the other hand, it was observed that he played happily enough with them after school, without fear. Was it the
teacher? No, he liked the teacher. This searching for answers
went on for months without anyone discovering what was
keeping this child out of school.

For a short while, following the November episode, Milo
consented to go to school if his mother accompanied him.
She sat all day long in the basement, and every five minutes
Milo ran out of the classroom and down the stairs to make
sure she was still there. He continued to refuse to go to school
unless she remained with him in the school building. In response to repeated questioning, Milo would only say, "I don't
know why I can't go to school, but I won't go till next year."

The above is the Presenting Problem, which was all that his
parents and teachers were able to see of him. No one looked
at him in "profile" to find out what it was he was *trying to accomplish* (his purpose). The parents did not see *themselves*
as the "other end of the stick." They were squinting through
the keyhole and seeing only his refusal to go to school. In
other ways they regarded him as a very satisfactory child and a
credit to their efforts. Unless the profile of his whole behavior
is drawn up, there isn't anyone who would not be puzzled!

When we do a profile and dehypnotize ourselves from the
presenting symptom, we find a number of other things. Milo
bit his nails and pulled at his sleeves. He was never a good
eater, although he drank milk well. He could never be told
anything by his mother. If she tried to tell him anything, he
yelled back and shouted at her. Whippings had done no good
in these situations. He showed much jealousy of his younger
brother. Though Milo was reserved, his brother was described

as a "kissing bug." Observing Milo's jealousy, the parents made a special point of kissing him. If Milo was refused anything, he became wildly angry. He resisted going to bed on time and demanded to stay up later than his brother. He commanded his father to play cards with him.

Both the father and the mother were completely devoted to these two sons. The father even borrowed money so they might have extra toys. Lacking money for baby-sitters, the parents never left their children or in any way became independent of them by having a life of their own, as adult human beings. Their way of life was geared to the level of their children. Though both boys played well enough with other children, neither of them had begun to turn to the outside world for emotional satisfactions from their age-mates. The parents and the children were preoccupied emotionally with one another. And in addition, the two boys were caught in a competition as to which one could get most attention from the parents.

This situation had been present from the start. Why did Milo wait until November of his second year in school to break loose? The trouble really began the previous August when the father was confined to the house with an illness and had to sit all day in a chair. His greatest delight during this period, and a compensation for his illness, was the behavior of his younger son. This little Kissing Bug took the opportunity to go to town! He spent most of his time swarming over his father, fondling and kissing him. In their complete contentment with each other, both of them lost sight of the world around them.

Hindsight is always perfect! Looking back, it was easy to see that this upset the balance of power for Milo. His enemy (brother) had captured the stronghold and was occupying it —completely. The parents had been and were entirely unaware of this until the profile was constructed for them.

Thinking back, they then remembered that Milo had become more aloof and distant as his brother had become more successful. Instead of asking for ice-cream money, as had been his custom, he now put his brother up to asking for it, as one who approaches the King's Favorite to get indulgence from the King! When it came time for him to go to second grade and leave brother behind, he began to resist the idea of school, which he had liked formerly.

During the months when brother had been getting the march on him, capturing the father, Milo had done things that had made him less and less popular with his father. Several times he was slapped for his bad behavior. This served to discourage him further and to enhance the success of his brother. Now it is possible to see why he felt that he dared not go to school until the following year, when his brother would be old enough to leave the home, too. In the meantime, he felt he had to remain home to make sure that his brother did not also steal the kitchen sink!

How he endured school from September until ten minutes of three one day in November, we shall never know. What caused the dam to break then and flood the countryside, we shall never know. Jealousy is like an ulcer that eats through in its own good time. Somehow that particular day was significant. Though the father returned to his job shortly afterward, Milo now was on equal footing with his mother and brother —home all day, to gather up whatever sweets she could furnish. With this new weapon at hand, Milo found that he received more attention than his brother had ever had! Both home and school went on their knees to him. On the few days he did go to school (with his mother in the basement) butter would have melted in the teacher's mouth, too! All the big boys were warned away. Whatever he did was highly praised. All this—and heaven too! Milo was not to be tempted from it lightly. He succeeded until May, when the light was turned full on for the parents.

When the total situation was illuminated the parents were aghast. For the first time they saw the full situation in which they had been living and realized to what degree they had molded their sons into becoming clever rascals. They realized that the younger boy, as well as the older, had devised unique techniques for gaining a tyrannical hold—especially on the father.

When the parents saw that they were the Big Game that had been hunted and trapped, they decided they would no longer be the victims of either the Kissing Bug or of Milo, with his "school-bell fever." They knew they must free themselves so their children could likewise be free of them. The path to growing up was now open to all four of them!

THE CASE OF BERT—THE SCARED LITTLE
TOUGH BOY

Bert was eight and a half years old. He can best be described as an Intelligent Little Stinker. He was sure death to any and all little girls. He hated them! As a third-grader, Bert was demoted and threatened with explusion because he had deliberately pushed a little girl down a long flight of stairs. Bert's whole conduct record in school was of this caliber. More than that, he was below grade in most school subjects, although he was considered to have a high I.Q. So, on the occasion of this stairwell episode, the principal of the school informed Bert's parents that he could not remain in school unless they did something immediately about their son's behavior.

This was the mother's Presenting Problem. She also included her own complaints, which were that Bert's facial tic and his eye-blinking almost drove her crazy, that he had temper tantrums and used bad language, and that he did not get along with his brother and sisters or with children in the neighborhood. The Presenting Problem is like the visible part of an iceberg. An iceberg is one tenth above the water level and nine tenths below the surface of the water. As might be guessed from the part thus far presented, we must be prepared for a picture of serious family disturbance. And we can be sure Bert had countless ways of keeping the family on its ear every minute of the day.

In addition to Bert there were three other children in the family—a brother two years older and two baby sisters, aged one and two. The mother waited hand and foot on all of these children. There was not a moment of the day or night that she set aside to call her own. Her four children squabbled and fought endlessly. Both she and her husband were forever screaming at the children to be quiet or were trying to quell their riotous behavior. They had no life of their own and no fun. It is not to be wondered that Bert's mother sat on the edge of her chair and that she appeared overanxious, tense, discouraged, and unhappy.

It *is* to be wondered, though, that this mother expected Bert to be self-reliant. She had never allowed either him or her other children to become independent. Immediately following the birth of her two little girls she had begun to feel especially burdened by Bert's demands on her, and gradually she had become more and more annoyed with him. Any resistance she made to his demands only made him fight harder for her attention. It became a vicious circle as Bert struggled to gain her unwilling interest!

How did Bert manage to annoy his mother, to say nothing of his father? He refused to allow his parents to go out at night. He would at no time be left alone. He would not dress or undress alone. Although he was very jealous of his older brother, he tagged him like a shadow. He would not go alone into the room they shared or go to bed until his brother did. He demanded to have the same things his brother was given —and then some. If his extravagant demands were denied, he stole. He couldn't stand the attention his mother gave his baby sisters. This led him to treat all little girls viciously by pushing them, banging them on the head, or spitting on them. He accused his mother of hating him. To get her attention he blinked his eyes and distorted his face. He had a passion for knives. Whenever he became angry he pulled out a knife, although his parents hid all knives and could not discover how he came by them. The violence of his temper frightened both his parents. If the boys in the neighborhood picked on him, he fought back with a "foul mouth." He had a vocabulary of filthy words that would shame a stevedore!

We do not need to go on listing things about Bert. We can see that although he thought he was strong, he was really very weak. He fought frantically with every infantile weapon at his command. He believed that his two baby sisters had stolen his mother's love (attention) from him. If we watch only what Bert does, we see that his behavior has a language all its own. His behavior says, "You may wish to be rid of me, but I shall make sure that you cannot overlook me. I can do this easily. I shall be a *bigger baby* than the babies. I shall try to destroy all little girls, wherever I find them, since they steal attention away from me. I want my mother to wait on no one but me. No little girl is going to steal my crutches. I shall cut them all down with a switch-blade knife!" All this, and more, his behavior says. At any rate, he acted as if he felt this way.

Bert's violence paints a vivid picture of his great fear of losing support and of being overlooked. He did the only thing that he understood. He hung on to his mother because he had never been weaned from her. Her other children clung to her, too, and in this respect were as ill-prepared to face the world alone as was Bert. The mother ignored this fact. She wanted only Bert's Presenting Problem (the most annoying symptoms) removed, and she discontinued treatment after the sixth interview because the most bothersome symptoms had disappeared. By this time Bert had started to behave better in school and was improving in his academic work; had given up his passion for knives; was making better adjustments to his brother, sisters, and the neighborhood children; went to bed alone; and did not scream his head off if she went out. However, at this time the mother herself had no full awareness of the extent to which she had crippled Bert as well as her other children.

The purpose in presenting this case has been to highlight the consequences when children are allowed to continue "eating at the breast," so to speak, and are never weaned emotionally. When such infantilism is sponsored, consciously or unconsciously, parents are eternally enslaved by, and involved with, their children. They have no time to maintain an interest in each other, as man and wife, or an interest in the outside world. The over-all situation is not improved until parents re-establish some interest in each other and together find a way to move independently of their children. If parents fail to keep in contact with each other and with what goes on in the world outside their home, their children have no respect for them because they are such nonentities. When parents fail to create lives of their own, their children *canabalize* them!

THE CASE OF CARL—"DUMB," LIKE A FOX!

Carl was an only child of eleven. He was in the triple-zero class at school. If there had been a lower class in his school, he would have managed to be at the bottom of that one! Even the "experts" regarded him as a stupid boy. The Presenting Problem was the school, of course. Because he had been assigned to a special Special Class for Backward Children, he had to travel some distance from home to school. The trip involved a bus change. The mother made the trip twice a day with Carl, since she was convinced he could never make it alone. Both parents were humiliated and ashamed that they had a "moron" for a son. There was no doubt in their minds of this fact. Everything Carl did proved to them that he was definitely not bright.

If we sat and glared at his academic record, as all the others had done, we might have agreed with them. But even this boy could not hide his real intelligence under the pretense of stupidity. In the development of the profile it was evident that it was another of those "now you see it, now you don't" cases. His cleverness in manipulating his mother into doing as he wanted her to do revealed his brilliant insight and perception of her weakness. Carl was definitely a *fox!*

His technique was that of a fox. When a fox has isolated a chicken from the flock, he gets it into the open field if possible. The chicken never takes its frightened eyes off the fox. The fox walks around and around in a wide circle, and the chicken keeps turning its head in a circle, watching, watching, watching, until eventually it gets so dizzy that it falls down. Then the fox makes his catch. Our boy, Carl, circled his mother in this way—endlessly—and caught her every time!

The development of the profile exposes his foxy tricks very well. They are enough to make anyone dizzy just reading about them! The mother had been ill with high blood pressure for many months before Carl's birth. He cried for three years after birth. As a result he developed a hernia and wore a truss. Then he got grippe and developed skin allergies and hay fever. He was afraid of everything and clung only to his mother. Countless times a day he would say, "Mother, I love you very much, do you love me?" He would insist on an answer.

Carl was sent to a private school at the age of six. If anyone spoke harshly to him, he vomited. He came home filled with "fears." He refused to go to camp with other boys. Once he had a small accident while playing ball. Thereafter he made a big fuss over every little scratch and demanded all kinds of care for it. If children in play pointed a toy gun at him, he acted terrified. This led the children to make great fun of him.

Carl wouldn't make any effort to chew his food or to suck milk through a straw out of a carton, as was the custom at school. He chewed on the straw instead of sucking the milk through it—this being the same Carl who could not chew his food! He pretended not to be able to suck on a Life-saver candy, and this led his mother to plead with him "just to try." The father resented his monkeyshines and tried to force issues. Vomiting put an end to father!

At times Carl would pretend he had "helpless hands," walking around with his arms extended in front of him and dangling his hands as if his wrists were broken. He did this whenever he chose to avoid certain tasks. For instance, he would refuse to button his coat. He demanded that his mother clean his fingernails. Although he washed his face, his wrist became weak when it came to washing behind his ears or combing his hair. He would button his shirt but find his hands too weak to tie his tie. He couldn't possibly find enough strength in his hands to cut up his meat, although he was as big as his mother. In school, he tricked his schoolmates as well as his teacher into doing things for him, such as opening his milk bottle. If his parents took him to a restaurant, Carl pulled food out of his mouth to embarrass them. No matter where he went in public, he touched everything much as a little infant does. Given an audience of any kind, he acted silly. His mother was so humiliated by his public performances that she tried to hide his inferiorities from eyes that might be watching. Out of shame, she kept trying to cover up his apparent helplessness, which led her continuously to increase, rather than decrease, her overprotectiveness.

The more overprotective the mother became, the more Carl refused to do anything, lest the rich rewards of his unfair taxation be cut off. If his mother defaulted in any way, he punished her by vomiting. He talked at her constantly whenever he was near or with her, asking the same silly question a hundred times and demanding that she answer. If she refused to answer, he would sometimes kick her or be otherwise abusive and then ask, "Are you afraid of me?"

Is there any need to go on describing the endless ways in which this inventive boy dominated by using stupidity as an exemption? The only mystery is how his parents or teachers or anyone else could have imagined him to be suffering from lack of intelligence! They could not have believed this if they had considered just three things, amongst others, that he did: he could tell time perfectly, he read the sports pages, and had learned perfectly all the tricks of baseball.

Every effort was made to prove to Carl's mother that all the signs had been misread. An effort was made to show her how to become more independent of this son so that he might become independent of her. In fifteen one-hour sessions it was possible to show her what might be achieved. Within this period of time Carl managed, with encouragement, to accomplish the following: he learned to ride on a bus alone and make proper change the first time he was allowed to do so; he began to do all the shopping for groceries for the family, with never a mistake in the items or the change of money that was involved; he went to the barber shop alone; he learned to make his bed; he went to school alone; he combed his hair and managed his own tie; he ceased vomiting when denied something; and he commenced work in a sixth-grade arithmetic book.

By this time the school year had ended. This boy, who had been unwilling to be apart from his mother, enthusiastically went off to camp for the summer. This mother, who had been afraid to trust her son out of her sight, went on an auto trip with her husband.

THE CASE OF HELENE—THE "BEWITCHED" PRINCESS!

Helene was nine years old and, if anyone cares, she had an I.Q. of 130. She should have been in fourth grade. But where was she? Well, that is the Presenting Problem. She was in a special class devoted to *nonreaders!* You may well ask how in the world a child with an I.Q. of 130 can be so far behind other children her own age.

A second part of the Presenting Problem, in addition to the school failure, was her exaggerated fears and terrible nightmares. She was in the habit of waking her parents as often as three times a night, screaming in terror and wet with perspiration. Each time this happened, they had to sit with her and calm her before she went back to sleep. The school failure and the nightmares were the only part of her total behavior the parents "squinted at." They would have been satisfied with her if these two difficulties were removed.

Without the profile of her behavior and the home situation, it would have been difficult, if not impossible, to understand her failures—unless we were to postulate some kind of horrible monsters creeping around in her subconscious! Fortunately, it was not necessary to invent them. The "monster" that was giving all the trouble was her little sister, who lived

in the home and not in her "unconscious." For six years
Helene had been an only child. The sister was born just about
the time for Helene to start to school. This meant she had to
leave the "fort" in the hands of the newly arrived enemy. It is
not surprising that she left her mind (soul) at home, though
she took her body to school.

Both of the parents were highly educated and put much
stress on academic prowess. They were overanxious to see that
their children had every possible cultural advantage. They
read a story to Helene every night at bedtime! Why should she
learn to read? In addition, there was a housekeeper to serve
her, as well as grandparents who pampered her. She was
thrown on adults for company and stimulation, since there
were no playmates living nearby.

Helene used baby talk. She was timid in nursery school and,
as a result, was shoved about. Until five and a half, she wet the
bed. She demanded constant attention and service, both day
and night. She was afraid of the dark. She dreamed of being
"outside" and of trying to get into her sister's room. She daw-
dled dressing and undressing. She complained about everything and cried easily. She refused to go to the toilet alone.
She was constantly afraid, and always blamed someone else
for any mishap. Children at school referred to her as a "privileged character"! She wiggled constantly. She teased endlessly
for things. She clung to a doll or teddy bear much of the time
and made a distracting fuss over it. She chattered incessantly
and made trouble about eating. She wanted to have her
own way and showed a general attitude of resistance. There
was constant jealousy and rivalry, of course, between Helene
and her little sister. Her sister, though a baby, constantly
needled Helene.

Helene was quite ostentatious and even appeared proud of
the many things she "could not do." It was as if she spoke of
money in the bank! Which it was, to be sure. There never was

a more transparent case of will-not. All of her movements showed that it was her purpose to act like a baby and get attention. She actually expressed it in words on several occasions, when she said, "I always wanted to be a baby before my sister came." But her parents did not realize that this ambition was the root of all the difficulty.

Fairy tales are full of stories of the beautiful young Princess who falls under the spell of an evil old witch, disguised as some innocent person. The witch changes the Princess into a toad or some defenseless creature, in which form she remains until rescued by the young Princess. In the case of Helene, the baby sister had a hypnotic influence over her. The infant, at birth, got the center of the stage. This is a "magical" position and one to conjure with! Our "bewitched" Princess tried to invent "countermagic" by out-babying the baby! By such means she hoped to usurp the position of the little sister. The parents, who were frightened of her failures, fell easy victim to her domination. Thus our Bewitched Princess was able to rule the roost from her "self-created lowly position." It paid her to *fail!*

The full-length mirror provided by the profile cured the parents of "squinting at" two dramatic symptoms and made them aware of the total picture in their home. Being intelligent people, it did not take them long to un-witch the Princess! In short, they began to live together on the more matter-of-fact basis of common folks with common sense. As a result, Helene soon found that it was more fun to work and play with her age-mates than it was to work so hard to keep adults in bondage.

The parents of the children in these four cases are not dissimilar to many parents today. Many parents are inclined to see only the symptom or the kind of behavior that has caused them to lose face with their neighbors, the school, or someone

else whose good opinion they value. When their failing children expose them to criticism, they come to resent them.
They seek a quick remedy or a magic formula that will remove
or suppress the particular aspect of their children's behavior
that has caused them the most pain or humiliation. They
hope they will be given Ten Tiny Techniques for Curing
Thoughtless Child Tyrants. It does not occur to them that
there are no such short-cut techniques.

Since parents themselves have been so misled and so misin-
formed, one can scarcely blame them if they see the symptoms of their children as serpents to be destroyed. They are
burdened, weary, and disappointed. They want to hold up
their heads in their community. So it is only natural for them
to seek some way of getting relief from their own situation vis-
à-vis those around them, rather than seeking ways of improving the over-all situation and the behavior of their children.

How can one expect parents to see problems in terms of
total relatedness when they have been led to look "inside" the
child? This has focused their attention on a single symptom
and resulted in their ding-donging on that symptom, night
and day. Let's just consider the symptom of bed-wetting as an
example. The whole atmosphere of the home and all the conversation in the home eventually revolves around wet sheets!
Even though the family physician or pediatrician may assure
the parent that there is no organic basis for this manifestation, he goes on hum-drumming as if the child couldn't control his bladder and as if that were the only thing he couldn't
control! This is what we mean by squinting through a keyhole. If a parent would get up off her knees and stop squinting, she might see such a manifestation as only a small segment of the whole infantile panorama the child presents.

We have frequently attempted to help a parent see the
whole problem by means of the following tidbit of conversation, which we always say in the child's hearing:

"Now then, Mother, your problem isn't so difficult. This ten-year-old boy of yours likes to sleep in a wet bed. So tonight you can make it easier for him. When he goes to bed, accompany him to his room with a glass of water. Before he goes to bed, pour the water on his sheets for him. Then he won't have to work so hard to be a baby. Don't you see what he is trying to tell you? He is trying to tell you that he remembers when you were more concerned with him than you are now. He wants to get back in the Diaper Derby. Don't talk any more, Mother. . . . ACT!"

The mother may not understand what we are saying to *her*, but her ten-year-old boy usually gets the point very well!

We carry on this conversation in the hope that either the parent or the child will stop pivoting around on a wet bed sheet. This pivoting around is similar to the "courtship dance" that African jungle fowl execute. In this dance, two fowl engage in a silly kind of sidewise motion, each reacting to the other's motion. While the dance continues, neither is free to act independently of the other. A parent and a little bedwetter are like this. Unless one or the other can be influenced to act independently, instead of *re*-acting dependently, the dance goes on and on without stopping!

Our next chapter presents an approximation of the usual around-the-clock dance that goes on between some parents and their children. It shows infantilism at work on a twenty-four-hour basis. It is a composite case of the more frequent things about which parents complain. You can substitute your own pet grudges in place of those we have described . . . and the meaning will not be altered in any way!

23

INFANTILISM AT WORK–
A RECAPITULATION

When we find a mother cutting up meat for a nine-year-old boy, we begin to grow suspicious. Then we find that he makes a fuss if she fails to trim off every speck of fat. Our cloud deepens. We discover this boy is using these bits of fat on the meat as if they were weapons to start a war at the table for the subjugation of the whole family, and this is so aggravating that the right of others to an enjoyable, peaceful meal is denied them. He is the undisputed monarch. We know that we will soon discover in what other ways the family submits obediently to this nine-year-old's tyranny and exploitation.

We must interrupt at this point to say that we cannot, nor should we want to, put "old heads on young shoulders." A child of three, a child of six, and a child of nine have vastly different potentialities. We should expect them to behave according to their age level. A child of three can hardly be expected to do a competent job of cutting up meat. A child of six might, and certainly a child of nine can do it. If he is not doing it by nine years of age, then we must suspect that we have an indicator of persisting infantilism—at least in this area.

Now that we have this meat evidence, we must make what might be called a shrewd guess as to the dominance-submission pattern our nine-year-old boy has worked out between himself and those around him. But as yet it is only a guess. It is time, though, to do a full-field investigation of the whole twenty-four-hour period of the day and night. If our guess is right, we shall find this boy is oppressing, enslaving, demanding, and disturbing at numberless points throughout the day and night in order to hold his parents on a leash, as one chains a dog. To confirm our guess, we must begin with the time he is supposed to get up and we must follow him around the clock. This will give us a profile of his characteristic day in the family. Once we have this profile, we may compare it with the profile of a self-reliant child of the same age. All of us know at least one child somewhere who has been trained to, and has learned to, act his age. And so—to the profile!

Comes the dawn. Mother and Dad get up, bathe, dress, get breakfast, and go about their tasks. Our Hero isn't awake. He must be wakened so that he can get to school on time. Mother goes to his room and pleads with him, as if on bended knee and with a sob in her voice, please to get up at once. She should, of course, have arranged for him to have an alarm clock to set and to use to wake himself up. At his age he is capable of a responsibility of this kind. Instead of getting up, Junior rolls over and, with one eye squinting, half-sleeps. Mother makes three more trips, getting increasingly angry each time. At long last, when he sees that she is about to hit him, he scrambles out of bed. But he does not dress. Instead, he sits on the side of the bed and dreams. Mother yells again. He puts on one sock, halfway. He takes time out to dream again or fiddle with his model airplane. This piecemeal process of dressing-sitting-dreaming-toying goes on until his mother, exhausted and out of patience, drags him to the breakfast table.

At the table begins the "battle of the bulge"! "To bulge or not to bulge"—that is his question. Can he annoy his mother more, he wonders, by wolfing down everything in sight? Or can he annoy her more by making her think he intends to starve himself? As he toys with these questions, Mother interrupts him. "Please, darling, eat your breakfast. You need the vitamins. They'll make you strong. And if you don't hurry you'll be late for school," she pleads. Now his energy is diverted to a resistant movement. He must show her who is boss in the family. He looks sullen. He takes a sip of milk. He dallies with his fork. He takes another wee sip. This continues until there is no time for Mother to stuff down his gullet the cereal, toast, and other things she has worked to prepare, because the last moment has come and he should be leaving the house in order not to be late for school. He dashes to the toilet, vomits up the half glass of milk, and Mother ejects him through the door toward school. Until he returns from school in the afternoon she is free to recover from her nervous collapse and to get ready for the tougher battles still to come!

By midafternoon Mother begins to gird herself for what she knows is about to happen. Her nerves are tightly wound when the door slams. Our Conquering Hero has returned from school. He rushes pell-mell into the hall, having dropped his cap on the threshold for Mother to pick up sometime later. He should pick it up? Are you kidding? He proceeds to dump his books in the umbrella stand. He carefully puts his overshoes on the piano. His coat finds its way under the table as he grabs a handful of cookies from the cooky jar after leaving his baseball mitt next to the eggbeater, where his mother is trying to prepare a cake she is going to bake for dinner. He hurries to the living room, scattering cooky crumbs and candy papers on the carpet. He draws up the most comfortable chair, turns on the television set, and sprawls in a coma-like state smack in front of the screen, with his dirty shoes up on the upholstery!

He maintains this trance although Mother may scream, beg, nag, threaten, and make gyrations like a whirling dervish in an attempt to persuade him to get her some milk at the corner grocer's or empty the garbage or get washed before Father comes home or "do his schoolwork before it is too late." Each request is followed by silence or refusals from him. She should ask him to do these things? And then Father does arrive. But he's not noticed. Father gets washed and drags up a straight chair on which to sit wearily until dinner is ready. Our now Exhausted Hero resents being called to dinner and finally almost has to be picked up bodily and dragged to the dinner table to be fed. While there he complains about: (1) the interruption of his television program, (2) the food his mother has prepared, (3) the bad treatment he got in school, (4) the mean way the kids next door treated him when he hit their dog, (5) the bus driver's refusal to wait while he finished the comic-book in the candy store, (6) that dope elected to be president of his class, (7) how he hates reading, writing, spelling, geography, social studies, grammar, arithmetic, sitting up straight, paying attention, and, well, anything else he can think of to complain about. Father and Mother sit through all this while their ulcerous stomachs churn, and without any opportunity to communicate with each other.

There is more to come. Their boy presents his list of demands. He lost a book on the playground and it must be replaced. He broke a boy's glasses, scuffling in line, and they have to pay for them. He wants an English bike instead of the new American make they just bought him a month ago. Someone stole his baseball bat when he left it lying on the front steps and he has to have another for tomorrow's game

in the sand lot. The neighbor's boy has a dog and he wants
one, too; in addition, he must have a tank of tropical fish and
a parakeet because they are being discussed in Science. No,
he will not be fitted for any new suit because all the fellows
wear only dungarees and that's what he wants! He will not
look like a bum if he wears them to school!

By this time his parents have finished the food on their
plates but he hasn't started. They begin to cajole him, and
they lose another half hour of their precious short evening
trying to get a few scraps of food into him. As soon as Mother
starts taking the dirty dishes to the kitchen and Father goes
to get the evening paper on the porch, he slips like a pinched
watermelon seed back into the comfortable chair before the
television set. After Mother has finished the dishes, the real
battle of the evening begins: to get him to study (?) his
school assignments. Father locates his books in the umbrella
stand finds the homework, but Son complains that he does
not understand the lesson. Why should he, when he paid
about as much attention to his teacher's explanations as he
pays to what his parents say to him? With a parent on each
side of him re-explaining, he dozes until they are worn out.
When *they* have learned the lesson and are now too exhausted to keep their own eyes open any longer, the lesson
ends. And he has slipped back again in front of the television
set before his parents can close *his* books and put them where
they can find them for his emergency exit the next morning!

His parents are not allowed to see the television program
they want to see, so Father reads the newspaper and mother
looks over the PTA bulletin. They have to recharge their
bodies for the final battle of the day. They still have to get
this boy of theirs into the same bed from which they had so
much trouble, only that morning, extricating him! They
know enough to start this struggle at least a half hour before
they expect him to make the first move toward the bathroom.

After all, they have had long experience. During the next half hour there are attacks, retreats, sabotage, excursions and alarms, diversionary tactics, feints, sallies, and all kinds of undercover work. At long last, their son is badgered into the bathroom. It takes twice the energy to get him out again! He still has to walk the "last mile" to the room where he sleeps. By this time the parents' main hope is to reserve enough strength to stagger into bed themselves.

This is the profile of our Conquering Hero. With slight variations, it is repeated day after day. Each year it becomes more difficult. When this boy was an infant-in-fact, his mother diapered him, gave him his bottle, and popped him into his crib. She had some time and some thought for herself. Now, instead of his becoming less of a burden as he grows stronger, he becomes more of a burden. The kind of demands he makes become more difficult for his parents to satisfy, instead of less. His direction, instead of being forward, is backward —toward cradle days.

If we compare this profile with that of a self-reliant child of the same age, we see a dramatic difference. He is interested in doing all that he can for himself. He does not seek ways to make unnecessary work for others. He has pride in demonstrating to himself how much he is able to do unsupported. He finds no satisfaction in disrupting those around him just to force them to be attentive to him. He discovers ways to occupy himself rather than ways to occupy others.

The emotionally healthy child looks forward to growing up. He does not enjoy the situation of being small and relatively helpless. He finds a sense of achievement in being able to do things for himself. It gives him a certain self-respect and value each time he gains the courage and the skill to handle new situations. He is proud when he overcomes his fear of the dark and of staying alone. He likes to tackle things even a bit too advanced for him to prove his ability to figure things out. He is annoyed if anyone interferes when he is "tinkering" with a new idea or project. He likes to explore the unknown and take chances. This is the natural response of all young animals that have not been misdirected or damaged by wrong educational efforts.

The child learns from us by the way we live with him. If we are fearful, anxious, impatient, demanding, and otherwise infantile as parents and teachers, then we become a problem to him. A fearful mother may easily damage the growing courage of the child by picturing the world around him as filled with hidden dangers. Children are not apt to become more matter-of-fact than parents are, unless they have the good fortune to learn common sense from some other child or a teacher. The child becomes the other end of the stick as he lives with his parents. The limitations of their own imagination, courage, resolution, may become his limits, too. Parents who try to save their children from all disappointments and frustrations only damage them. In such cases, their children will give up too easily when they are faced with independent tasks that others cannot do for them, such as schoolwork, eating, thinking, sleeping, and many other things.

Adults who are emotionally mature lead their own lives and are not unreasonably distracted by their children. Such parents do not feel their children to be a *burden*. As mature adults, they plow their own straight furrows and do not zigzag trying to keep up with the unnecessary infantile demands of their children. When the child makes unreasonable or unnecessary demands for adult service or attention, these parents allow him to bear the frustration of refusal. His temper tantrums do not move them. In time, the child learns what he may expect and what will not be given him. He learns to create for himself much that he thought should be given him freely. The refusal of his parents to accede to his unreasonable demands stimulates his self-reliance and inventiveness. In this

way parents live with children AS THEIR FRIENDS AND NOT AS
THEIR SERVANTS!

ANOTHER LOOK (AT THE SAME OLE PROBLEM)!

The outside world gives *nothing without payment!* And no
reasonable grownup wants to get something for nothing. The
earlier children learn this fact of life, the more surely will
they grow up to be good fellow men. The conditions of survival in the home should always be substantially the same as
those in the outside world. Then the child will move naturally toward adulthood without feeling shock when he discovers what is expected of him outside the home. But if the
home is a hothouse of pampering created by pampering, anxious parents, then the child will not be prepared for the
colder emotional climate elsewhere.

The relationship between parent and child must be one of
mutual respect. Parents who behave like servants to their
children are treated like the flunkies they are. The child spits
down on them. Pampering or pushing parents never understand why their children do not respect them. But they are
treated by their children as inferiors because they have acted
as subordinates. The child has set the pace and they have followed. Why should their children regard them as important?

The parent who has lost his position of respect and authority with children must regain it both for his own sake and for
the sake of the proper development of the children. Much of
the servitude into which parents have fallen is so habitual
that they have to be furnished the equivalent of a full-length
mirror in which they can see where their submissiveness is
sticking out for the child to exploit. Once they are able to
see themselves *as the child sees them,* they are prepared to

stop giving him their false support, and he will have to find a way of standing on his own feet instead of theirs. When parents refuse to be crutches, the child becomes sure-footed!

In other words, parents *at all times* must exercise their right to freedom and the pursuit of happiness, as the only sure way of avoiding the condition of slavery. Rights that are not exercised are soon stolen by those who would like to profit from them. Children are very watchful! They are as persistent in this respect as a dog that is determined to sleep on the new sofa. Although the dog may not crawl up on the sofa when we are around, everyone knows what happens when we leave the house. We find his hair on the new sofa when we return. Parents who do not hold on to their full rights will soon find their children in possession of them. We propose now to furnish a full-length mirror in which a parent can see where he has lost some of his rights to the child. This is in the form of a questionnaire. It pinpoints a number of apparently small things that parents may be doing or enduring in relation to their child, without being aware of their real importance. If they find that their child is in the habit of behaving in any one of these ways, then it is an indictment of them, not the child! To repeat: the parents are on the other end of the stick, and the child could not be doing what he's doing unless his parents made it possible by subsidizing such behavior. These are the things they have told him "a thousand times not to do." But they themselves did not stop doing what they should not have been doing!

The proper way to use this questionnaire, then, is for parents to look into it and see what they are doing to the child, through their subsidies. It is not to be used as a way of accusing the child. Parents should remember at all times that the child's infantilisms are but the mirror image of their own infantilism. Parents, then, are the *ones who must grow up first* so that the child himself can grow up! In short, parents must give up what they are doing mistakenly if they want their child to give up what he is doing. It is that simple. It is unreasonable to expect the image in the mirror to behave differently from the person who stands before it! That happens only at Coney Island!

With this questionnaire it is easy to review or audit a typical day of the child in the home and school. From it, parents can make a profile of all the infantile behavior they find. Then their work is cut out for them. They can begin at once to work on themselves to rehabilitate themselves into human beings instead of zombies who are obedient slaves of an infantile child. By the time they have overcome their own subservience they will find that their child has grown behaviorwise according to his age level.

QUESTIONNAIRE

FOR ANY AGE GROUP BEYOND THE INFANCY PERIOD—

Which means the Child, the Bed-wetting Soldier in the Army, or Grandma!

(A Full-Length Mirror for Parents)

I. Since when has there been cause for complaint? What kind of situation (psychic or otherwise) did the child find himself in when his failings were first noticed? Was it the beginning of school, the birth of another child, an illness, divorce of parents, or some other new factor?

What Did You Do About His Manifestation?

II. Does the child display timidity, reserve, envy, jealousy, clumsiness, dependence on others when eating or dressing, washing, or going to bed? Is he afraid of the dark? Does he speak clearly for his age? Is he too closely attached to either parent, grandparents, some other relative, et cetera? Does he make hard work of doing simple things?

How Do You Habitually Handle Him in These Situations?

III. Does he cry out at night or wet the bed? Is he bossy to weaker children or to stronger children? Is he teased and derided? Does he want to sleep in his parents' bed? Is he vain of his looks, clothes, hair, et cetera? Does he bite his nails, make faces, and do other things of this kind that annoy adults?

Are the Methods You Are Using Making It Possible For Him to Continue Such Infantile Behavior Rather Than Challenging Him to Be More Independent?

IV. Does he make friends easily? Or does he molest and annoy people or animals? Does he hoard and refuse to share fairly? Does he whine and beg for everything he sees?

Have You Outlined for Yourself What You Are Doing About Each of These?

V. Does he like school? Is he punctual? Does he lose his books, assignments? Is he fearful of tests and bad marks? Does he get excited at the prospect of them? Does he waste his time or daydream, clown, forget his assignments, refuse to pay attention, and otherwise disturb his teacher and the class? Is he critical, arrogant, indifferent to the teacher? Does he ask for help from others and stop working when they stop helping him? Does he want only to play?

In What Ways Are You Taking Up the Slack When You Should Be Letting Him Bear His Burdens?

VI. Does he show much rivalry at home and in school? Does he tattle on others or blame them for his failures? Does he show a tendency to deprecate others?

Have You Made Any Headway in Teaching Him to Mind His Own Business?

VII. Does he show any ambition for his future? Or is he vague and unrealistic about what he expects to do when he grows up?

Have You Given Him Any Reason to Think That He Must Grow Up Some Day and Support Himself?

VIII. Does he consider himself put back and neglected? Does he give up easily unless he is praised and encouraged all the time? Does he like to pretend he is the baby who must be helped? Does he pretend stupidity when faced with difficult tasks? Does he claim lack of talent for school, for work, for life? Is he servile, stubborn, rebellious?

How Have You Let Him Believe That He Should Have the Spotlight All The Time?

IX. In what areas does he show ability in performance? In what ways is he a help and not a burden?

You Can Take a Bow for These!

X. Does he keep things in order? Hang up his clothes, comb his own hair, take his own bath, cut up his own food, eat without disturbance, go to bed and get up without a struggle, care for his own toys? Does he sit properly and not wiggle or act irritable?

How Did You Do This? Take Another Bow!

XI. Is he able to entertain himself when he has no play-mates, or does he nag you to think of things for him to do? Does he expect you to amuse him and be his play-mates? Does he prefer the company of adults to that of his age-mates?

If He Is Not Able to Entertain Himself, Who Has Been Entertaining Him All the While?

XII. Does he nag to get what he wants? Or whine and cry? Does he have tantrums or does he sulk when refused? Is he "deaf" when asked to do something? Does he insist on coming to the table with unwashed hands? Does he eat in a disgusting manner? Does he demand special foods? And then often not eat them?

Do You Walk Out on His Act, or Listen to His Soap Opera?

Of course, in the questionnaire not all the ways are listed in which a child can manage to disrupt, burden, annoy, or sabotage his parents or teacher by acting at cross-purposes to the needs of the situation. But it should be remembered that any such behavior is *purposive*.

WHAT HAPPENS IS INTENDED! The purpose is to enslave and engross the parents, teacher, or whoever happens to be in charge of the situation. The child is trying to set up a nursery situation such as he had in infancy. He has lost his courage and imagination to go forward toward mature self-sufficiency. His best way in which to accomplish his purpose is to be a burden and not a help. Thus others are obliged to give him the beloved attention he seeks so avidly. He devotes most of his intelligence to the accomplishment of such infantile goals.

The main concern of all of us who live with children any time, anywhere, is to become wise enough to keep out of the traps they set for our unwary feet. These traps hobble us, but more than that—and worse—they hobble our children!

24

FIFTY THOUSAND YEARS OF
EVOLUTION CAN'T BE WRONG

The average young mother with her first baby is frequently a comic figure. You would imagine she had invented the idea in the first place. From the manner in which she treats her infant, one gets the impression that she feels that no one in the world had ever had a baby before. However, by the time she has had her third or fourth child, if she has that many, she scarcely takes time out for her confinement. By that time she has learned that babies are almost indestructible—one might say that Old Dame Nature was not silly enough to wait for the human race to learn how to take care of babies. There would be no human race at all if infants were as easily destroyed or damaged as most young parents believe them to be. Nature did such a good job on the human infant that it takes years of determined mismanagement on the part of parents to spoil a child.

In the recent past it has become fashionable to picture the parent-child relationship as such a delicate, fragile thing that a single misstep might ruin it. Parents have been led to believe that a sharp word in anger, a slap on the bottom, a bit of neglect, a fleeting frown, or almost anything could produce an impression on a child that would ruin him for life. If this were true, the human race would have destroyed itself while it was a-borning. It would not have reached even the stage of living in caves and hunting the saber-toothed tiger.

If human beings could be destroyed so easily, they would not have developed and multiplied until they had dominion over all the earth. Quite the opposite is true. In the beginning, the very nature of life forced man to look after himself in order to survive. In those early, early days of harsh reality, parents did not live in a quandary as to whether to cut off Junior's food allowance if he was too lazy to catch his own, or at least help catch the family food supply when he was old enough to do so. They chose to let the little beggar go hungry until he was willing to contribute to the survival needs of the family. By watching other people, Junior soon caught on to these needs and to the rules of the game. He didn't have too much choice, because in those days a condition of scarcity existed for everyone. When Little Irresponsible would not eat, parents didn't spend their own food budget rushing him to a pediatrician or a psychologist to unearth the reason!

In this respect modern parents have been the victims of a sad kind of education that has led them to believe they dare not trust their own good horse sense in matters relating to the rearing of their children. That is why this book was written. It is our belief that we cannot, as human beings, avoid all mistakes. Just because some parents have made mistakes, it is not the signal for *all* parents to abdicate their own judgment in favor of some outside Big Wheel who is supposed to know all the answers. Parents certainly should not hop from one fad to another, as Eliza hopped from one ice floe to another in crossing the river! Parents should not sit by, doing nothing, because they are in terror of doing the wrong thing —or wait for the latest bulletin from the child-guidance expert.

There is a great deal of difference between a problem that needs outside help and a problem that doesn't. You wouldn't

run to the doctor to have a mosquito bite bandaged, but neither would you depend on mercurochrome to heal a ruptured
appendix.

Parents are held responsible for their children and therefore should not abdicate their own inner authority in favor of
some outside authority unless the situation really gets out of
hand. They must overcome their fear of making mistakes and
begin to rely on their own fundamental common sense for
direction in bringing up their children. And what is common
sense? The cave man and his mate knew that answer. They
knew that their children had to be made strong and independent so that they could slay the saber-toothed tigers and
make their skins into clothing to protect them. They understood that survival as an independent entity is the goal of life.
Survival depended on each child's growing up to do his share.
Whatever did not help survival was not encouraged—and
only self-reliance helped survival!

If survival, in our modern age, means that each parent must
become an expert on child guidance, by learning *all* the
dodges and quirks in the latest editions of manuals on psychiatry and psychology, then the human race is doomed to
extinction. There could be no other outcome, because the so-
called experts do not agree even among themselves as to what
is the Right and Only Way to diaper the baby or to do anything else for him.

Let's face it! There is no one-and-only Right Way to do
anything. There are as many ways to get a result as there are
people. Parents have only to find their own sensible way to
make their children self-reliant and self-sufficient. What we
have written here is by no means to be taken as the Only
Right Way. But experience has convinced us that it is *one* effective right way. That is why we, as authors, have not written a "How To Do It" book, for parents should not try to
dodge the responsibility of finding their own way, by rushing

to a bookshelf. It is a parent's job to discover what to do with Junior when he won't eat what is served for the family. Personally, we would eat and let him go hungry. Our figuring would be that there are only three reasons why a child would go long without eating: (1) because there was nothing of any kind to eat, (2) because he was too sick to eat, (3) to spite his parents and show that in a general contest of wills he could outwit them.

The purpose of this book has been to give parents a birds'-eye view of the over-all problem so the main outlines would come into perspective. Or it might be considered like the map of a country, by means of which a traveler may proceed as he wills toward his destination. A family may have any number of members in it, from a newborn infant to grandparents about to die. If they are under the same roof they need a map or a master plan in common so that they may live together in a way that will not sacrifice one age to another. If there is such a plan, then one group is not suppressed by or dominated by the other.

This point of view is in contradiction to much that has been promulgated in recent years about the "special needs" of certain ages. If a household is run on a special-need basis, the whole household must be run differently for a child of one to four years than it is for an adolescent child. And neither of these two ways would be right for dear old Grandma, who may be living under the same roof and who may have her own special needs. Under such circumstances, the house quickly becomes an unrealistic never-never land. Books with recommendations about special needs assume that parents are miracle workers who will provide all these needs for each age group. However, these books fail to say who is to provide for the "special needs" of the parental providers when they are harassed and exhausted!

This book is about the needs of parents as well as the needs of children. In the productive years of their life, parents have their own jobs to do. They should not be occupied running around foolishly providing special needs for everyone—except themselves. After all, the full responsibility for the family is ultimately centered on them. It is not right that parents should be stuck with responsibility if they are not to keep as much authority as they need to do the job.

None of this means that parents cannot learn anything from books on child guidance, psychology, psychiatry, medicine, or other related material. That should be obvious from the fact that we've written this book. However, it definitely does mean that parents should not abdicate blindly to outside authorities. Many years before anyone ever thought of special needs, the human race managed to exist on the face of this earth. It is much more important for parents to work out a proper general outline for a common existence based on live-and-let-live in family life than it is to worry about any one member's "id" or "super-ego," whatever they may or may not mean. If they do exist in reality, cave men probably had them, too. Therefore, "ids" and "egos" cannot be fatal in and of themselves!

Parents need only bear in mind the fact that Old Dame Nature is on the side of survival—that she didn't intend that the human being worry himself into death. Worrying-to-death, however, is what parents can look forward to these days if they keep adding to their fears of this-and-that or see everything as dangerous.

Certainly, not everything in the field of psychology and child guidance has been wrong. The swing away from the hickory-stick school was in itself a good thing. However, much of it has not squared with common sense. Parents, in self-defense, have to learn to discriminate in this respect. As an example, we might reappraise the dictum that stressed that it is dangerous to the personality of a child to prevent him from doing everything he wants to do. Adults were urged not to indoctrinate a child in any way. It was implied, if not expressed in so many words, that the little child would "just naturally" find all wisdom inside himself. Parents were cautioned that if they stopped a child, they might plant the seeds of a neurosis that would sprout and bloom in later life. As a result, acres of wallpaper and freshly painted walls (to cite only one consequence) were ruined in homes where parents dared not stop a child in the expression of his little ego! However, if he started playing on the window ledge, the same parents yanked him back quickly enough to save his life. If it was bad for his little ego to stop his scribbling or crayoning on the walls, it must have been just as bad for his little ego to stop his playing on the window ledge!

Such nonsense came from a lack of understanding of what a neurosis is and what it means in terms of function. A neurosis is no deep, dark thing, as was commonly imagined. It is a lack of any will to be productive. In other words, a neurotic person wants to continue throughout his life in his original condition of infantile dependence, in which condition he can continue to consume goods as well as services without having to produce anything of value in exchange for them. It is an "I will not produce" rather than an "I cannot produce," as the neurotic claims.

Parents would not lose their way in the rearing of their children if they didn't lose sight of the target or the goal at which they are supposed to be aiming. Parents who allow their children to mark up the wallpaper, for instance, or break the furniture, and are afraid to stop them, are parents who lost sight of their target somewhere along the line. Their target, in this instance, should have been training their children to understand that in this world of ours as it is, and as it will continue to be, they have no right to destroy at random, according to their whims, the products and possessions of other people.

Parents who understand that life means to be a help and not a burden will rear children who also understand this fact. They will invent their own techniques and play by ear, so to speak, as to the manner in which they should teach their children not to lean or depend on others. They will know that if they do not allow their children to lean on them when it is not necessary, their children will learn to help themselves.

A farmer knows the effect of climate on the growth of plants. He knows that if the climate is wrong, his plants will not grow properly. All parents, whether or not they know it, set up a "climate" inside the home. Fortunate indeed is the child whose parents have set up a climate of self-sufficiency.

When this is the over-all climate in a home, it will apply equally to each and every age from the youngest to the oldest, including Grandma. When all are governed by the yardstick of self-reliance and group welfare, even Grandma will not whine if the family goes off to the movies and she has to entertain herself.

But woe unto the child reared in a home where parents have set up a climate based on "special needs." Such homes resound with demands and bickering. Each member expects, as his just due, that his special needs be considered and catered to. But he neither expects nor intends to pay for what he demands. It is in these homes that one finds parents running to supply everyone's needs—but their own.

To all PARENTS ON THE RUN—a final message:

Stop running. Stand your ground. Stop begging from your children. Do not let them beg from you. It is not what your children want but what they are trained to do on their own that will enrich their lives. Remember that as the tree inclines, so was the twig bent. Live on a self-sufficient, self-fulfilling, and productive basis yourselves, and your children will live likewise. This is the way to enrich them. Then you will enjoy them and they will enjoy you.

SEEK AND YE SHALL FIND

A Bibliography

Those who wish to know more about the philosophy and the concepts on which this book is based should read these books by Alfred Adler:

What Life Should Mean to You, Grosset & Dunlap
Understanding Human Nature, World Publishing Company
The Education of Children, Greenberg Publishing Company
The Pattern of Life, Cosmopolitan Book Corporation

Other concepts of this same type may be found in the following books:

Guiding Human Misfits, Alexandra Adler, M.D., The Macmillan Company
Your Nervous Child, Irwin Wexberg, M.D., Albert and Charles Boni
What It Means to Grow Up, Fritz Kunkel, Charles Scribner & Sons
Fundamentals of Adlerian Psychology, Rudolph Dreikurs, M.D., Greenberg Publishing Company
The ABC of Individual Psychology, Phillipe Mairet, Greenberg Publishing Company
Corrective Treatment for Unadjusted Children, N. E. Shoobs & George Goldberg (Educators), Harper and Brothers

Those who wish to learn some answers found in other cultures should read:

Patterns of Culture, Ruth Benedict, Houghton Mifflin Company
Coming of Age in Samoa, Margaret Mead, William Morrow and Company

Those who disbelieve that humans were born to cooperate should read:

On Being Human, Ashley Montagu, Henry Schuman, Inc.

Those who live with seriously handicapped children should read:

Born That Way, Earl Carlson, M.D. (a spastic), John Day & Company

Those who mistake the WORD for the THING should read:

The Tyranny of Words, Stuart Chase, Harcourt Brace